HOW & WHY

GOVERNMENT

FAILS US

Can We Learn From a Book?

This book details how our government functions without regard for the negative ramifications of its actions. While this was written a few years ago, many of its references have been retained through an editing process because they still apply in today's world. It may also be interesting to take a look back into our colorful history.

TABLE OF CONTENTS

INTRODUCTION

Government, in theory, is supposed to provide services that the population is not able to easily supply for themselves. Unfortunately, what has happened is that politicians have become So, corrupted by the purse strings of corporate

America that they are no longer able or willing to serve the people to any great degree. Laws tend to favor the few and ignore the many. This state of affairs has come about because Congresspersons have their own Prime Directive to follow... and that is getting reelected. Fortunately for them, there are So, few voters who are paying attention.

The Secrecy Factor

When the politicians are not directly covering up their own corruption or obscuring their personal agendas, they may be actively engaged in promoting a veil of government secrecy which appears to be increasing in its rate of occurrence. This is in no small part due to a lackadaisical press that benefits from their symbiotic relationships with those who are in power. This secrecy occurs when…

* Presidents invoke Executive Privilege
* incriminating documents are classified
* politicians exaggerate national security issues
* the State Secrets Act is used to prevent information from being given to the courts

Since the courts can view evidence in chambers that is sensitive in nature, why should we prevent them from doing this when alleged state secrets are involved?

Administrations tend to engage in a policy of no disclosure is better than some. The less information that is revealed to the public, the less the politicians can be criticized for, or perhaps jailed for. We suffer from government-imposed secrecy in a myriad of ways. There are more than 1.000.000 people with the authority to classify information, or about one out of every four hundred men, women and children in this country. How many of these people do you think mark a document classified to save their own behinds?

Short of having the Freedom of Information Act (FOI) invoked, politicians are relatively free to operate in an environment which may be impenetrable to the public. And little is being done to prevent this according to a coalition of 67 organizations (whose findings are rarely reported by the press) that are dedicated to increasing government openness.

Apparently this predilection towards secrecy has not been lost on state governments either. Since 2001 the state legislatures have passed more than 50 bills that expand their executive powers, impose confidentiality based on dubious federal regulations or programs, and close public meetings for alleged security reasons. Just what kind of security needs do the states have that the public does not have a right to know? Can you name even one thing, other than an occasional personnel consideration, that justifies a closed session?

There is even a veil of secrecy for those who donate big bucks to Presidential libraries. So, why would these benefactors care about a President who is deceased? And why should they care if their financial participation is known? Well, if you believe that these libraries do not act as propaganda organs for those companies and individuals who have benefited from close Presidential relationships, hmmm. Maybe you believe that knowing who donates is not important. Maybe you think that they are just being charitable and have no quid-pro-quo agenda. Maybe you are asleep. These libraries should not be used to promote editorial content if their implied mission is the unbiased presentation of historical materials. They are however not So, detached from outside influences. They are in the business of portraying a President's term in the brightest light possible. And that includes obfuscating dubious associations with others who may not want the true light of day cast on their activities. In addition, the aggrandizement of Presidents tends to obfuscate the unprofessional dealings of all politicians, as with the concept of innocent by association.

Freedom of Information

The FOI act was enacted to open up the government to greater public scrutiny, but this concept is frequently being thwarted by an effective tactic of administrative delays. Officials in want of privacy are becoming adept at throwing up procedural roadblocks that prevent divulging what they are up to. If you would like to know more about this subject go to... www.openthegovernment.com

One aspect of government secrecy that puzzles me is that we all have to live under this same system of rampant dishonesty. Our legislators are not exempt from the repercussions, just as we are not. They may initially achieve some short-term personal gain while they are in office, but that ends at some point in time. So, why do they feel the need to corrupt government for everyone, including themselves, their children, and grandchildren? Are they that myopic? The obvious answer is reelection rules. Even when we expose governmental misdeeds there is little penalty for bending the rules or breaking the law.

When agencies are asked to provide relevant data regarding a particular subject under investigation by Congress, some of that requested information may be deliberately left out. An investigation of the treatment of terrorist prisoners at our base in

Cuba is a case in point. After the initial inquiry took place it was revealed that the CIA had destroyed videotapes of the persons who were tortured to extract information. Allegedly this was done to protect the identity of those agents involved in conducting the questioning. Forget that their images could easily have been obscured to prevent identification. So, the CIA broke the law by not retaining the tapes, and then they went on to fabricate a lie about their justification for doing so. Wouldn't you think that someone might be punished for this? Once again, apparently not. Later there was another investigation of the original investigation whose only perceived purpose was to embarrass the administration and was not intended to right a wrong. Bringing the felon(s) to justice rarely occurs to Congress, and only on the odd occasion do any of these public servants lose their jobs for breaking the law.

On those few occasions that congressional committees have been authorized to investigate some controversial issue, they invariably end up being little more than window dressing. In other words, they are designed to look like they are doing something constructive when in fact they are doing nothing. This action is undoubtedly intended to diminish Congress's do-nothing image. Are you fooled by this opera? Did you even know that there was one on stage?

Government Missteps

Government policies from time to time have catastrophic repercussions. In the distant past the denial of resources to the South prior to the US Civil War was a precursor of the same type of prohibition that was used against the Japanese. It consequently brought them into WWII. We limited their access to the raw materials that could be used to further their expansion plans, and they vigorously objected to that restriction.

Will Rogers, humorist: *"I don't make jokes. I just watch the government and report the facts."*

While the appeasement policy toward Germany's aggression by Neville Chamberlain of Great Britain was a catastrophic failure, it should not have colored our national posture as much as it seems to have done. Since that ill-fated lesson of not relying on negotiations occurred, we have participated in four major wars with little to show for it in the last two… Vietnam and Iraq-Afghanistan-Pakistan. How long will it take for us to balance force with intellect. When President Carter went on a fact-finding trip in 2008 and talked to Hamas there was much criticism, especially from Israel and Israel promoters in this country for his engaging in that effort. How does communicating with an advisory get such a bad rap anyway? Don't we have a State Department with this very mandate? To top off an imperfect Mid-East policy, the US and Israel have failed to negotiate in good faith with Iran, Hamas, and Palestinians. We continue to set preconditions which are routinely rejected. Some countries enjoy poking the bully in the eye.

Jimmy Carter, President: "Since Clinton left office there hasn't been a single day of good-faith peace talks between Israel and the Palestinians orchestrated by Washington. It is terrible and tragic and counterproductive to avoid communicating with people who disagree with us."

Palestinian Oppression

First let me say that I am not a bigoted Jew basher. I have had many acquaintances and good friends over the years that were Jewish. My opinions only reflect a lack of respect for some of the unfortunate attitudes that are manifested by government of Israel and some Israel supporters in this country, and nothing more. For years there has been an ongoing Palestinian problem that has not been properly addressed by this country, Israel, or other nations around the world. The Palestinians quite rightly do not want to be oppressed by the Israelis that surround them on nearly all sides, and they will occasionally lash out violently against their landlords. Because their homeland is being boycotted, they are at the mercy of Israel in nearly every direction. They have no…

* trade route highways that are not subject to closure without notice or justification
* ports that they are able to ship and receive goods from
* real industry of their own (who would order a product with an irregular delivery schedule?)
* permission to collect taxes to pay for fire, police, teachers, and infrastructure (as if that is any of Israel business)

In affect Palestine is a reluctant colony of Israel, and they have been subjected to harsh penalties when putting up violent resistance against their treatment. Because of these circumstances, 42% of the people who voted in their 2013 election cast their ballots for Hamas, the armed resistance. This was surely because the Palestinians have seen their country routinely taken from them by…

* Israeli settlements (some 200 of them)
* roads within their country that they not permitted to cross even to get to their own fields
* a forty-foot-high wall that separates them from sections of their own lands and is manned by checkpoints.

It does not take a genius to see that what is going on here is theft of land on a grand scale in the name of Israeli security… not to mention a theft of a people's dignity. How would you react if the states which surround yours...

* decided to prevent the free exit and entry of goods and people between your state and its neighbors
* forced some of your people off of their native land in order to build new subdivisions for themselves
* prevented you from having a tax-paid government to manage your affairs independently

You too would be furious I presume.

In 2010 an advocate for Israel stated on a talk show that giving back territory to the Arabs was the worst thing they could do. Oh really? Maybe he should take a look at what giving up nothing for decades has accomplished. I guess that using someone else's land as a war buffer is deemed to be a valid excuse for domination. The act of negotiating a lasting peace does not seem to garner much interest with Israelis. What may account for the conflicts that the Israelis have with their neighboring countries seems to demonstrate the way that they live in the past. Their national psyche of insisting on remembering the Holocaust may act as paranoia which prevents them from realistically dealing with the present. In addition, some Orthodox Jews use the Torah to justify their attacks on their neighbor. This is how a rigid, religious, mindset works against peace while encouraging the wrath of other Middle Eastern countries.

In 2011 the Palestinians petitioned the United Nations to recognize them as a state. President Obama voiced strong objections to this matter. Apparently he feels that it is more important to placate the Israelis rather than to give a colonized people their right to self-determination. Haven't we been down this road for far too many years with only poor results to show for it?

Jordan's King Abdullah: "Israel must choose between living with the mentality of Israel-the-fortress or living in peace and security with its neighbors."

Why We Participate

A side effect of the Palestinian Problem is that the US has aligned itself with and financially supports the Israeli's repression. Unlike the more balanced European reporting, our press is shameless in their biased and limited information on this subject. As a result, we are seldom privy to the inner happenings of the conflict, and we are then supplied with disinformation that is more sympathetic to the Israeli view then is it to the reality of the Middle East. As a consequence of this propaganda, the attitude of our nation is skewed in the direction where the Middle East countries barely tolerate us. The likely outcome of this situation is...

* the world's continued dislike of Israel by moderate countries
* intense hatred of Israel by Arab countries
* more world terrorism

Is it worth that? Do we really think that some countries desire (So, they say) to see Israel erased from the map is for no reason? And much of the generally negative attitude toward them rightfully rubs off on the US for its complicity in this matter. It has been many years since we experienced the cold war and the degree of hatred toward the US that the Soviet Union was able to whip up until recent years. Being a balanced, responsible, and not overbearing member of the world community could be a workable answer to the conflict, but we don't seem to get it. My argument is not meant to castigate Israel as a whole but to identify the forces within its borders and ours who knowingly and through gross ignorance are preventing a Palestinian solution. From all appearances this tragedy is being perpetuated by a powerful political coalition (and their supporters in this country) with land to gain. Wars and conflict are always about economics after all. And this seems to be a case of take something and give nothing.

What is it about Israel that induces the US to support their colonialism to the tune of billions of dollars per year in military aid and handouts?

We would surely not consider this level of funding for any other country. Are they our buffer? We berate Russia, China and others for their repeated human rights violations, but remain strangely mute on the Palestine issue. Are we ignorant of what is happening, or is there something else at play that only the insiders know? How did having a discussion of this subject become So, untouchable?

Once again we have positioned ourselves as the ugly Americans.

The Viet-Iraq Wars

If we are to learn anything useful about politicians from our history, the war in Vietnam should have been a training ground. For those who remember the events of the 60s, they taught us that...

* Americans like to trust their military leaders in spite of their often-demonstrated lack of veracity
* Presidents cannot be trusted to tell us the truth when they have a hidden agenda, which is far too frequent
* high level advisors in government survive their terms, often without integrity, because they are in the business of saying yes
* the generals and the CIA will parrot whatever the White House demands until they are out of office, at which time a touch of integrity may strike

* the regular troops in the field are never listened to because they might have honest, derogatory opinions
* it is extremely difficult to control or oppress a people in their homeland because they have much more at stake than the invading foreigners ever will - look at how the Afghans (with our hardware) were able to force the Russians out
* brute force is not a substitute for brains

In order to justify the war that <u>we</u> started in Vietnam we were told that...
* a patrol boat attacked (really?) our much larger ship, and that is what justified the 'police' action for us
* we needed to make the world safe for democracy
* if South Vietnam fell to the North, the Russians and Chinese would spread Communism throughout the area and the neighboring countries would fall like dominos
* people would be oppressed and millions would starve

What we were not told was that we wanted to develop Vietnam's coastline for oil. Well, we lost the war, and oops, none of the above ever came true. When I think about the Vietnam War Memorial, I see the names of all of the dead soldiers that were carved into the marble slabs. Did any of them have to die for their country? I don't think so. In the war for pacifying Iraq we were again implored to believe that...

* they were building weapons of mass
destruction, and that is what justified the
invasion for us
* we needed to make the world safe for
democracy
* if Iraq fell to the terrorists they would spread
Islamic law and extremism through the area
* countries will fall like dominos

We were not told was that our primary
motivation was to secure the stability of Iraq's
oilfields. Maybe we should have lost the war (by
going home) and see what would have actually
happened. Since we are almost universally
disliked by Middle Eastern countries and
tolerated by some European countries, when we
are gone the Arabs will only have Israel to focus
on, which seems to be able to take care of itself.
If we went home, the militant's stated reason for
hostility (our invading their land) would be
neutralized, and perhaps they might even want to
get on with their lives. As it stands now, we are
the Great Satin', which is an idea that their
leaders utilize to rally millions of people to their
cause. No Great Satin, no rally! Or is that too
simple an idea for the pinheads in Washington to
comprehend. Obviously it was for the
Bush/Obama crowd. Because of kicking sand in
the eyes of Muslims for years it might be too late
to stop the violence in the Middle East no matter
what we do now. We gave the terrorists a reason

to die, and that fervor may not change any time in the foreseeable future.

Arab conquest of lands and people, which has been going on for thousands of years, has been replaced with a kind of religious multi-nationalism. It is not a single country that they represent, just one religiously minded group. We are in their lands, and they can be stirred up into hating us for it, just as they have always hated invading peoples. So, why don't we get out of Arabia, mind our own business, and let them kill each other instead of us? Spending hundreds of billions of dollars in Iraq, Afghanistan and elsewhere has no obvious justification. The predictable results have been...
* thousands of US soldiers dead
* tens of thousands of US soldiers wounded
* a near depression
* a decline in our world stature

Denial of Culpability

For generations the US government has lived under the shadow of disrespect with many second and third world counties. Even when the Soviet Union was in its most repressive heyday, most of the world's non-European countries were leaning toward or actively supporting the USSR. Why? Since the end of WWII, the US has shown a need to flex its muscles when dealing with others. And that penchant is not welcome in most of the world. Today Russia and China have very little to gain from any serious confrontation with the US, yet they continue to maintain a belligerent attitude towards us. They also, engage in proxy wars by supplying those terrorists that serve to diminish us. This occurs because...

* they like the revenue from their selling war toys
* we have never learned the art of humility, conciliation, and cooperation with other countries whenever we perceive that our interests are at stake
* the need to win at any cost is what makes us lose

Our politicians foolishly support these bullying behaviors that are made inevitable by our unwavering support for big oil and the military-industrial-complex. Then we portray ourselves as the good guys, to the disbelief and distain of the countries of the world.

Instead of focusing on undermining corrupt dictators, we fight wars for oil, while all the same time squandering that precious resource and other critical assets in the process. So...

* Could this act be any more counter-productive?
* Could its narrow-minded promoters be any more ignorant?

* Is there anyone left in Washington who has not been subverted by the lobbying process, to the detriment of this country?

Our difficulties around the world are largely self-inflicted bruises.

Denial of Reality

When I worked at IBM many years I thought it would be fair that incomes should be taxed at 90% or more on all earnings above about $400.000, in that day's dollars. My friend was vehemently opposed to this idea because he did not want to subvert his opportunity for wealth, the so-called promise of America. When I checked in with him a couple of years after moving on to consulting work in California, he was still a clerk, presumably holding onto his unfulfilled dream. In the meantime he was paying a greater share of the tax burden then was equitable. The possibility (or fantasy) of greater financial success, not unlike thoughts of winning a jackpot in Las Vegas, are what can keep people in their place and the wealthy in the place they would want to be. So, some fifty years later I sometimes wonder where my old friend is and how much of the apple he actually got a bite of. And did he ever think again about a fairer distribution of wealth.

Let me make one thing perfectly clear. Redistribution of wealth is not like playing Robin

Hood of Locksley. Wealthy people are wealthy, to some degree, because the tax and business systems are skewed in their favor in countless ways, and conversely against the poor and middle classes. Can you really believe that Bill Gate's business efforts are worth perhaps ten million times what his housekeeper may make? As an interesting aside about Bill, were you aware of the reports that his acumen involved halfheartedly developing a windows system for IBM while he worked on one of his own? And of course, we know which one prevailed. My curiosity about this has always been: how did IBM let that inexcusable lap happen? Who was minding their store?

Anyway, promoting the redistribution of wealth, such as with a more progressive tax rate, can be an equitable method for adjusting take-home pay without resorting to the disincentive nature of socialism that is gaining in popularity. Unfortunately, the trend has been in the direction of a regressive tax structure since the Kennedy administration and JFK's mentor John Maynard Keynes became *the* authority on taxation. The disincentive of a social programs state has been created as some form of compensation, but it's a poor balance.
Both Bush administrations had seen that their already rich buddies got an even bigger slice of the pie, all with nary a peep from those who are most adversely affected by the steady stream of

give-a-ways to the rich, i.e. the lower and middle classes. They seem to be satisfied with the small bones that they are occasionally thrown their way. This is what happens when people pay no attention to Washington and continue to trust that their interests are being taken care of.

Thomas Jefferson, President: A government big enough to give you everything you want, is strong enough to take everything you have.

How often have you heard someone say that they would vote for a particular politician because they happened to advocate a particular tax cut or some other money give-away? These are the same folks who cannot seem to understand just how small their portion of a targeted tax cut is actually is. Nor do they pay attention to the need to pay back the debt, or how inflation diminishes their earnings. It's incredible how easily duped the public is.

A common misconception (thanks to the disinformation provided by the wealthy) is that the rich deserve their obscene wealth in spite of gross poverty and a shrinking middle class.

Then there is the problem of where the interest payments on our national debt end up. Of course, they go to the lenders. And that often means foreign governments that use it as a safe haven for their oil or cheap-labor riches. Over time some of this money comes back to the US in the form of business purchases. What that implies is that the interest on the money we borrow to support our huge debt can end up with those countries that are buying pieces of America. The money goes around and around while our assets diminish, and our debt increases. Care to buy a Danish Budweiser or a Chinese nearly anything?

Milton Friedman, economist: *"If you put the federal government in charge of the Sahara Desert, in 5 years there'd be a shortage of sand."*

Global Pollution

When I was a kid I wondered where all of the smoke went from fireplaces, factory chimneys, and leaf burning (my favorite chore). It was carried up into the sky, and then what? I figured that the sky was So, large that must be able to endlessly absorb the smoke. Today we should be aware that anything which is sent into the atmosphere will reappear down here. The world has a balance where nothing is lost or gained. The earth is a closed system where matter can only be…
* reduced (oxidized)
* converted (combined or broken apart)
* absorbed (taken in by plant life, oceans, etc.)
* sequestered (buried)

…but it can never be destroyed.

What is sent up into the air may fall back to earth as harmless ingredients due to interaction with the sun or with other molecules. At other times we end up with pollutants that return to harm us. Has anyone been to parts of California or China lately? Similarly, when we dispose of our waste into dumps it is only temporarily out of sight. The materials will eventually…
* dissolved by contact with other garbage or molecules in the soil
* form gasses that enter the atmosphere
* be broken down by rainwater
* leach into the earth to be transported about by ground water

While current waste storage technology slows these processes considerably, it does not entirely stop them. Whatever is used to restrain the spread of our waste is only temporary since everything eventually degrades. Why do you think the residents of Nevada are So, opposed to accepting a nuclear waste depository?

Be careful what you throw away because there is **no away**.

Because we have had So, many quick and dirty methods for disposing of used materials, we have not stopped to consider the implications of those actions. When I was a child, my mom darned

socks and my dad repaired household appliances as necessary, etc. But today is a different story...
* we send our outdated electronics to the landfills rather than salvaging the materials
* manufacturing companies dispose of their byproducts into oceans, rivers, lakes, and streams
* for years Los Angeles dumped untreated effluent directly into the Pacific Ocean
* San Diego is still doing that, but to a lesser degree today
* ocean going ships may disposed of their unwanted materials (jetsum) at sea when no one is looking

While this environmental misbehavior may have slowed in recent times, it should be clear that we still live on a planet that is gradually poisoning itself. And we may not be able to develop an antidote in time to reverse the process. But as usual we twiddle our thumbs and are unwilling to take those actions that are required to resolve our contributions to pollution. It is always easier to spend twice the money later then it is to correct something now. Or is it?

Note: We and the planet are one - the proof is coming ever more quickly.

Defeating Solutions

At one time the Bay Bridge (Oakland to San Francisco) was scheduled to have mass transit occupy the proposed second deck. However, lobbying by automobile, tire, and oil corporations prevented this in order to sell more of their products to the increase in cars that were a natural result. Because of this mindset and the corrupting of public officials, mass transportation for the Bay Area never really blossomed in a way that would have prevented the glut of pollution spewing vehicles. In the 1940's the city of Los Angeles had an electric trolley system named Pacific Railway. A consortium that partnered GM, Firestone Tires, Standard Oil, and Mack Trucks purchased the railway in 1944. Shortly thereafter they dismantled the system to increase the market for their products, and this has contributed to decades of traffic congestion in the LA basin. In the 1950's a company named Alweg built a monorail system for the Seattle fair at no cost to the state. Their business plan was to have its ridership cover the cost of construction. The monorail was So, successful that it paid for itself in eight months. Later this company offered the city of Los Angeles a similar arrangement to build forty miles of monorail over its freeways. But the offer was rejected because of pressure from auto and tire manufacturers. It would have dramatically reduced the need for busses, automobiles, and the tires that they run on. In the late 70s, Texas oil companies were involved in buying up marginal rigs from small producers. Did they then use their newer techniques to enhance oil production, like water and steam injection or rock cracking by explosive charge? No. They capped the wells with cement to control an oversupply of crude. Then they bought up marginal refiners and stopped their production of crude oil to further reduce the supply. Have you noticed that the oil refineries have their 'previously scheduled' maintenance shutdowns at the times of increased demand in order to jack up prices? And all of these events occur under the red, puffy, noses of congresspersons who are elected to office to represent the public interest. The reality is of course that business interests and campaign financing come first.

Energy Solutions

The prevailing attitude in this and other countries has been to use as much fossil fuel as we may desire to power the world's economies because it is still relatively cheap and plentiful. Cheap, that is if we don't consider the environmental damage and the other indirect costs of that usage. Plentiful, if we don't look too far down the road when the supply will inevitably dwindle.

The downside to our current mentality, which believes that we have unlimited supplies and an unlimited time to develop alternative solutions, should be obvious. A few of them are...
* substantial pollution
* more greenhouse gasses

* increasingly adverse weather
* a dwindling energy supply
* escalating prices
* support for terrorism
* unnecessary military adventures
* reduced world security

There are, however, several long-term solutions available to us if we choose to implement them. While a few options may not be mature enough to put into production any time soon, a good number of them are. For example, this country is blessed with abundant wind at both coasts and in the Midwest. The electricity generating capacity of the heartland alone through the use of wind power would produce enough electricity to satisfy the entire country if we were to update the electrical transmission infrastructure (erecting a major network of new lines and substations to transfer that energy). While it would pose a significant expense, what is this outlay in comparison to the hundreds of billions of dollars that have been wasted in Iraq and Afghanistan? Are we just penny wise and pound stupid?

Lately the natural gas that is trapped below the surface in shale rock has been looking like a viable alternative to oil exploration. The immediate problem is a lack of regulation and a cowboy mentality on the companies that are retrieving this gas. The dangerous chemicals that are used in the extraction process have leaked into some water tables. But if that issue can be resolved we are in business with a longer-term, fuel source.

There is also, a virtually unlimited amount of mantle heat that can be converted into electricity from within the earth's interior. And the earth is not going to cool down in the next billion years. This is one hot rock we live on. We already tap this virtually pollution free resource where it is near the surface with geothermal generators in California and elsewhere.

If we chose to move forward with this technology there is engineering that would allow is to recover this resource economically everywhere except perhaps under the mountains. If we can drill for gas and oil miles under the sea, or have mines that are miles deep, we can do this as well.

As a recent technical bonus, we can now generate more power from less-warm ground water than was thought possible in the past. The bad news is…
* this would confront the existing infrastructure of coal, oil, gas, refining and delivery
* some gas stations would have to be abandoned or turned into electric or hydrogen delivery stations

* jobs disruption could be substantial as we convert from a petroleum-based economy to a renewable energy economy

The good news, if you can call it that, is that we will have to make this change in the future anyway as oil and gas supplies are depleted, terminated by hostile countries, or priced too high to tolerate. So, rather than postponing the inevitable and putting ourselves at risk, we should start working to avoid the upcoming crisis with its even higher cost. With that effort come the benefits of reducing pollution, global warming, and the military adventures involved in securing oil.

On a more local basis, new home builders can tap into the heat source under most home sites. Since the temperature of the ground is nearly constant some feet down, looped water pipes can be buried to transfer that heat differential, compared to the above ground, to help cool a home in summer and help heat it in winter. Short of the initial expense and the minimal water circulation costs, this is a free energy source. When compared to the cost of normal heating and cooling over time, the savings are substantial.

If you are building a new home, you might consider having your contractor build in an efficient wastewater heat exchanger. A great deal

of heat goes down the drain from showers and washers. There are also, contractors who can build homes which require minimum of heating and cooling through insulation. The greening of homes is relatively affordable technology, and it is here today. There is no excuse for not moving forward with it. We just have to insist on using this modern technology to...
* get off the grid
* realize long term savings
* reduce pollution with all of its obvious and hidden costs

The CAFÉ Standards

Because the human mind is not generally well-steeped in logic we can be fooled by clever manipulators. There is a genetic tendency toward being believers rather than being doubters. That wiring can and does work against us from time to time.

Doubters and skeptics are generally frowned upon (because they are different, another evolutionary trait) even though they represent important checks and balances against those who would deceive us. Apathy abounds when if comes to the critical examination of facts. This is part of the reason why scam artists continue to be successful in spite of the repeated exposures of their trade.

George Bernard Shaw, author: *"Accurate observation is commonly called cynicism by those who have not got it."*

Our willingness to be believers may not induce us to consider the implication of what we are told, and we may assign unwarranted credibility to the tellers. This would certainly be the case with the CAFÉ standards that were supposed to produce fuel efficient cars beginning more than 30 years ago. The government's initially stated objective was to create a progressively higher gas mileage average from each manufacturer over time. Who knew that over time would take the number of years that it has? In the meantime, the public may have settled into the notion that we are actually doing something about fuel economy, which the facts dispute.

The easiest way to cut your car's fuel bill in half is to buy a vehicle that gets twice as many miles to the gallon… Well, duh.

Prior to 2010 it was some ten years since the government installed a new mileage standard. There had been no changes in it during that time due to the lobbying by the auto industry. Even while automobile engines have become significantly more efficient over the last years (thanks to competition from Japan and pressure from California), some of the economic benefits have been cancelled out by the increasing bloat of the vehicles. A 4500-pound Cadillac of the past has now been converted into a heavier stretched Escalade.

Auto companies have learned that they only have to meet the mileage requirements and not exceed them. As a result, they have been busy catering to the shortsighted American appetite for size, which they helped to promote through advertising. Big is where the greater profit margins have always been.

Smaller cars with smaller margins are only built to keep the Japanese and Koreans from overrunning our market any more than they already have. Apparently winning the car sales wars with other countries is not a high priority in Detroit if it interferes with high profits. So, they buried their heads in the sand, presuming that all will be Well, if they just don't think about it now, to paraphrase Scarlet O'Hara's monologue in "Gone With The Wind".

Vehicle manufacturers in this country lack the incentive to change their scenario. Now the Japanese have been diving headlong into the large truck and SUV markets with their higher profit margins, which will leave Detroit where, exactly? How long will it take for them to get the message that quality and economy count?

While the manufacturers have been ignoring the future, we may have been telling ourselves that the CAFÉ Standards were accomplishing something. Could we be more wrong? The fleet mileage ratings from 1982 were virtually the same as those from 2006, according to the EPA... a statistic that is both unbelievable and unacceptable... with nary a peep out of the EPA. The years of window stickers, government bureaucracy, and false promises have amounted to nearly nothing, except of course for the wasted salaries of those who are employed to oversee this government/industry farce.

The clearest indictment of the auto industry is that after thirty years, the government is still managing fuel economy.

It is surprising to me how often automobile magazines and auto rating newspaper articles glorify excessive horsepower while ignoring its obvious downside. For the US public, power sells because that is what we have been indoctrinated to believe in for So, many years. There has probably never been an issue of the leading motoring trends magazine that has not feature excessive horsepower on multiple pages. One particular issue dealt with super cars that can be purchased directly off of a showroom floor that are reaching the 500 to 700 horsepower level, or nearly the same as race cars. With the top speed limit of 65 to 75mph on our highways, do we really need cars that can exceed that figure by 100mph or more?

Horsepower is essentially a measure of an engine's ability to burn its fuel quickly. Is this what we should be trying to achieve?

If engine technology hadn't improved dramatically over the last twenty-five years, the mileage rating numbers would be far worse. So, the expensive technology that we have created and pay dearly for with the internal combustion engine has been wasted on the increasing weight that has been added to vehicles.

Oh yes, did I mention that the alleged mileage ratings that are posted by the auto industry were somewhat bogus? Prior to the 2009 models, virtually no car got the miles per gallon that were displayed on the window sticker unless it was driven downhill more often than uphill. Some, like the hybrid Prius, got dramatically less than their posted numbers in spite of a carefully fostered impression to the contrary through advertising.

The people who run the mileage program have known of these discrepancies for years, and yet had done little to correct the testing algorithm. Neither have the auto industry or the politicians with oversight power. To the contrary, these are some of the same people that have prevented gasoline usage from decreasing.

When the mileage requirements first came out, ads were required to specify both the city and highway ratings individually because only the highway mileage was being advertised by the auto companies. Later a compromise was reached between the manufacturers and the government, the nearly meaningless combined city/highway rating that was used for a while. Now the Feds are letting manufacturers tout only the highway mileage again as if drivers didn't spend most of their time driving in the city. And I don't consider clogged freeways during rush hours to be a highway.

In addition to the above regulations, the Feds elected to completely remove all truck-sized vehicles from the ratings game some years ago, except for a few light-duty trucks. This means that the poorest vehicle mileage ratings are never disclosed to the public or figured in the corporate mileage ratings. Those numbers are not even revealed to us in the automobile magazines, much to their discredit. No doubt this is due to the fact that so much of their advertising revenue comes from the manufacturers.

Information that the Hummer, for example, had a city mileage rating only marginally better than a thirty-eight-passenger diesel bus is not in the public domain. And the manufacturers will not volunteer this data without pressure from Congress, which does not stand up to big business, and chooses to cave in rather than perform a service.

In 2011 the government proposed doubling the mileage requirements for automobiles and light truck and vans. But these new standards are not due to go into effect until after 2016, with heavy vehicles being exempt until at least 2020 and will then be phased in over five additional years. So, the worst of the worst are given the biggest breaks. All the while the industry has known that these targets were coming down the road and have done little to accomplish them ahead of the deadlines.

One last indictment against the auto industry is the decades of deceit involving the dealer sales system. No one who is paying even a modest amount of attention to this charade thinks that there is not something rotten in Denmark. Manufacturer suggested retail prices (as with clothing and many food items) are a fabrication that is manipulated by the car makers, dealerships, and their salespersons against the buying skills of the consumers.

Ads that tout prices below factory invoice are a prime example of this deceit. The so-called 'dealer cost' that may be presented to the public is higher than the actual cost to the dealer. This is because the manufacturers rebate a percentage of the retail price back to the dealers on each sale. Somehow this scheme may be used to keep the feds off of their backs for illegal pricing. So much for the fed controls.

How long will we continue to accept a system that is this corrupt before insisting on honesty? And the manufacturers do not object to this deceptive marketing because their primary interest is to sell cars any way they can.

Back to fuel. When the price of gasoline first rose to more than $3.00 per gallon after the Katrina hurricane a few years back, more people were driven toward economy cars than by any other effort that was enacted by Congress. That fact alone should make it clear that the bureaucracy has been thoroughly inept at lessening our reliance on imported oil or on reducing the greenhouse effect derived from that usage.

People will only change their buying habits when they are pinched in the pocketbook. So, rather that adopting a mileage standard that does nothing to curb demand, what we need to do is what the Europeans have done... double and tripled the price of gasoline as a way of punishing the biggest offenders and reducing the outflow of revenue from their countries. They still drive cars in Europe. But they also, drive a wider variety of smaller, more fuel-efficient cars, many with diesel engines. In fact, diesel cars have more than 50% of the market in Europe.

In 2011 Europe's mileage ratings averaged 35 miles per gallon vs. 22 miles per gallon in the US. Does that clarify what is going on with the auto industry? Since modern diesel engines are a way of life in Europe, 40 miles per gallon is a reality, not a fantasy. So, can we learn from their example, or must we continue to be enamored of the massive, excessively-power vehicles that have been indelibly pressed into our consciousness through advertising.

In 2010 there was only one manufacturer selling a diesel car in this country, and that was from a European company. US plans for building these engines are still years away, if they even remain on the drawing board.

About twenty-five years ago GM flirted with diesel engines. The problem then was that they elected to convert an existing gasoline Oldsmobile engine to diesel rather than using a sturdier, made-for-diesel engine block. As a result, they were smoky, noisy, hard starting, and short lived. A typical Detroit non-effort.

While a steep rise in the price of gas would undoubtedly have a disproportional effect on the poor, there can be adequate tax remedies enacted to manage that negative side effect. Europe seems to have dealt with the problem over gas prices which in some places exceed $11 per gallon. Are they that much smarter? A more appropriate question might be: are we that much dumber? If we averaged 33 mpg vs. 22 mpg, the price of gasoline could go up by more than fifty percent without costing a penny more.

Then there is the true price of a gallon of gasoline which is far greater than the pump price. Just as with the tomato picking that is done by the illegals and is subsidized in a variety of ways, we do not charge the full measure directly to consumer for the costs that are incurred with gasoline consumption. Chief among them are the military adventures that are employed to maintain our access to crude oil. Or are you under the impression that we had a benevolent interest in Iraq? If helpfulness were our true desire we would have employed diplomacy in the Middle East. Or perhaps we would have paid more attention to the life and death agonies that have been ongoing in Africa for years.

Rather than having the proposed mileage standards apply to each truck or automobile in a manufacturer's line, they apply to the corporations as a whole. The implication is that

Detroit can go on producing gas guzzlers as long as it manages to sell a significant number of high mileage cars to offset that downside. The Big Three mentality has always been to have the large, high-profit vehicles subsidize small, low-profit vehicles, and the government does little to change this mindset.

What do you think will happen to Detroit when the Chinese begin sending over small, Well built, high mileage cars to the US? Detroit is so locked into the big-car/big-profit scenario that they have no concept of any other game plan and may not be able to adapt this time around. The industry could all too soon learn a lesson at the expense of our nation when sales begin to drop like a rock... again. To make this point, the public is becoming progressively more interested in fuel economy as witnessed by the thousands of pre-orders that were make for the small, foreign, Smart car.

The got-to-have-a-truck mentality dominates blue color workers. The few tools that most of them use could easily fit into the trunk of a sedan or coupe. But how embarrassing would it be to show up in that kind of vehicle? OMG! We have paved roads to almost everywhere, don't we? Are $200+ tires really required to navigate occasional dirt or mud?

In 2015 Ford's answer to the mileage issue was to substitute aluminum for steel in some of their truck's body parts. Surely downsizing could have been an option, but have you seen a current compact truck lately? The ones that were built for a short while have transitioned into becoming So, big that one has to look closely to distinguish them from the full-sized trucks. Small would be wimpy.

Travel With Excess

If you are not towing a yacht or camper, do you really need...
* a 4.000+ pound truck to carry 100 pounds of tools (maybe) and a single occupant (If you are not convinced that this happens with regularity, just check the HOV lanes for the conspicuous absence of these vehicles)
* the extra weight of a dozen surround-sound speakers
* the weight penalty of a rarely used seven or eight passenger seating arrangement

Let's not pretend that 90% of the non-commercial, heavy truck, and SUV drivers are satisfying anything more their egos. In those rare circumstances when a cargo bed is required or transportation for seven is a needed, they could phone up a rental company and get one for the day.

My wife and I do a fair amount of carrying of items in our car, from firewood, to food, to appliances, etc. And this vehicle is a mid-sized, 2-door convertible. If we can manage our transport needs with our 'truck', So, can others with their sedan.

Maybe we should re-think the equation between our indulgences and the negative implications on the planet. I experienced an eye-popping example of vehicular gluttony on a trip to the Southern California coast. There was a torrent of massive, tricked-out SUVs barreling 60 to 70 mph down the Pacific Coast Highway's 50mph, intra-city Pacific Coast Highway with no concern that the signal light ahead was red. What about...
* teaching sane driving habits in driver's education?
* saving some of the finite gasoline supply for someone else?
* conserving the metals, plastics, and other materials that cars are made from?
* not acting like pampered morons.

Arizona is no exception to this foolishness. Try driving on Scottsdale Road in Scottsdale/Phoenix without being passed by vehicles barreling toward the next red light. Do they not get the connection between gas mileage and the stopped cars ahead? Are brake linings and gasoline that inexpensive?

Consumption Solution

After the $4-5 per gallon shock a while back, gasoline dropped below the $2.00 level and the automakers wondered what cars the public would be buying in the future. Perhaps they questioned…

* Can we still build our beloved, monster SUV's and trucks?
* Do we stop the R&D on electric cars?
* Does the public really care about miles per gallon?

People may care about the price of gas, but they do not relate to the mileage of their vehicles because they pay no attention to *those* numbers.

I think the manufacturer's questions about driver preferences could be responded to by expanding the gas guzzler tax dramatically, let's say with a $1000 tax for every mpg that a vehicle gets under 30 mpg. Then over time increase that number to 40 mpg and then 50 mpg. In this scenario, those who choose to buy a vehicle that gets 10-15 mpg would have to cough up an additional twenty to forty grand more for their foolish pleasure.

If the manufacturers knew that their customers would be heavily taxed on excessive consumption, the angst about whether or not to build large vehicles would be moot. As an ancillary benefit we would not have Congress's ineffective CAFÉ standards and all of the people that are paid out of taxpayer funds to oversee that boondoggle.

The point I would make about the energy problems, such as the diminishing crude oil reserves and the terrorist sympathizers who may control some of them, is this. There are generally simple solutions if we are willing to make practical, useful decisions. Perhaps it is a nothing more than matter of punishing the biggest offenders into submission. This method of crude oil control is more cost-effective than pursuing solutions promoted by an ineffective, corrupted bureaucracy. But don't plan on getting their support any time soon. Oversight officials are far too busy receiving there generous salaries to be even modestly concerned with efficiency or integrity.

Junk Cell Solution

In its infinite wisdom the government released everyone's cell phone numbers to telemarketers. Now we cannot only be harassed by these leaches on society, but we can also, pay for the privilege because these may be chargeable calls on your telephone bills.

There is an opt-out capability though. Just call 888.382.1222 from the cell phone that you want to be ad blocked. Oh, did I mention that this blocking does not apply to politicians when in vote gathering mode? Or the so-called charities that only pretend to be doing good deeds? And that this opt-out must be renewed annually?

BTW. If you donate to a charity do you know where the money actually goes? Does it go 100% to the children as with the charity set up by Danny Thomas years ago? A few of them put most of the money in the pockets of those who organized the 'charity'.

Backing up a bit, let me see if I have this right. We release the telephone numbers of all cell phones so that we can enable some government agency to exist in order to issue them and then enforce a blocked number list against the telemarketers. Is that a brilliant plan, or what? Well, it does happen to employee more people in a government agency. Say, isn't a department director's GS pay grade is based on the number of employees working under him or her?

The War on Drugs

The war on drugs has to be the most fruitless and counterproductive government intervention into people's lives since Prohibition was enacted in the 20's. This policy of many administrations has had the effect of immensely more harm than good by any reasonable analysis of the facts. What could be more irrational than a grossly expensive (tens of billions of dollars) and virtually ineffective effort to prevent the sale, distribution, use of illicit drugs? In addition, it occupies tens of thousands of government employees (both state and federal) along with their endless salaries.

One definition of insanity is: Repeating an action and expecting to have different results.

This has been a very long-lasting experiment, yet it has consistently failed to show any detectable signs of success. People can still get drugs if they want to... and they do want to. Overcrowding the jails with non-violent offenders apparently does nothing to change that equation.

We have spent decades of diverted law enforcement and wasted tax dollars on this thoughtless foolishness. And what are the tangible accomplishments that can be demonstrated for pursuing that folly? I don't believe it would be much of a stretch to say nothing. Actually, less than nothing would be more accurate if we take into account the immense human damage that this foolish confrontation with foolish pleasure has created.

While I can't easily get into the minds of those who are in charge or in favor of this 'war', here are a few possibilities of what they may be thinking...
* users are persons who do not deserve any consideration

* drug use is illegal, and jail time is what users should expect
* users are a drain on society in general, and should be punished

As for me, I can only express my anecdotal opinions about our war on drugs from what I read and see in the media since I am not out there in the trenches, nor am I part of the drug landscape. Apparently what we have is a great deal of holier-than-thou pontificating and an endless succession of worthless drug busts.

Any large quantity arrests are followed by the same, old, immodest press releases trumpeting their version of success, all of which results in...
* no reduction in the amount of drugs consumed
* a state provoked increase in crime
* overcrowded jails and their incumbent costs

Even more curiously, this unmitigated failure comes without any reduction in the DEA's massive outlays which might indicate that they are doing something right. On the other hand, we can mindlessly cut the critical funding for air tankers and firefighters that is desperately needed to fight forest fires. But the anti-drug budget rolls on virtually unimpeded.

From the evidence that is there for all to see (except those with blinders on), it should not be very difficult to conclude that nothing substantive has been accomplished, nor is any progress likely to be accomplished through this prohibition. It should also, be abundantly clear to anyone who cares to be objective that people will continue to obtain illegal drugs for exactly as long as they continue to desire them… not one second less, no matter what steps the government takes to mitigate their usage.

What appears to have been accomplished by the attempts at drug interdiction, though, is an environment where the drug sellers (as was also, with the history of alcohol prohibition) kill hundreds to retain their piece of the market. And they probably thank us for our repressive laws because it raises both drug prices and their massive profits.

The prohibition laws are thoroughly ineffective in dealing with drug demand, just as they were with alcohol a century ago. In fact, it can be argued that they are actually counter-productive because we tend to crave what we are denied. Just look at the college and high school drinking binges that have become a rite of passage for some.

If I am able to make this logical observation without any difficulty, why can't the boneheads in our government do the same thing? Well, one possible answer lies with the prevalent mentality of So, many that pleasure repression trumps common sense.

My take on the war on drugs does not imply that drugs are not or cannot be harmful, or that I believe that no actions should be taken to mitigate their usage. What it does demonstrate is that the drug enforcement agencies are employing unworkable tactics in their effort to eradicate drugs use, and that they are not able or simply not willing to make this determination on their own.

Is it possible that the feds persist in using unproductive means because their employment and generous salaries are more important to them? Is it possible that those people who are in administrative positions in government could be this self-serving at the expense of people's lives? Can the deaths of thousands be meaningless? Absolutely!

Some of the same arguments regarding the prohibition of drugs can be said about the past campaign against smoking. We artificially raised the purchase price of cigarettes dramatically through taxation, but this did not do nearly as much to discourage smoking as what the out-of-the-closet-non-smokers have accomplished with their efforts at reeducation and smoking restrictions in public places.

What the drug enforcement people do not understand, or more likely have chosen to ignore, is fivefold…
* making drug possession illegal encourages its misuse
* drug use is a status thing, Jack, because it is imagined to be cool and alluring, and it will continue unabated for as long as it is thought of as cool and alluring
* drug use can be, and often does become a debilitating addiction that should be treated as a medical issue when appropriate
* jails have not been shown to be anything approaching a solution
* the war on drugs is not free or cheap

We would be much more effective at stopping drug proliferation if we were able to convince the users that it is only the dopes that use dope. An advertising campaign which showed simpletons and losers as drug users might be effective at taking the mystique away from its usage.

Advertising slogans like "Your brain on drugs" may sound cute, but they are inherently meaningless (because they are disbelieved) and are therefore ineffective because they do nothing to attack the fundamentals of drug use, which are experimentation, entertainment, and rebelling against the system. Getting high diminishes people's concerns about any personal health issues that may be involved.

We need to take the glamour out of drugs. But most assuredly, we should not show our ignorance by jailing vast numbers of people for behaving naturally. We should also, reconsider the common belief that social problems can be solved by incarceration, and that the employment of more government employees, police, judges, and lawyers is a solution.

The difficulty with trying to promote this train of thought is that the current system is being promoted by these same government employees, police, judges, and lawyers. They either haven't enough common sense to find workable answers, or they have other agendas (like their paychecks) which prevent the use of realistic solutions.

Less dogma and more intellect could go a long way toward drug reduction, and that should lead to...
* fewer people in jail
* a subsequent reduction in the massive court and prison costs
* fewer crimes that are committed to support the artificially high price of prohibited drugs
* fewer dollars in the hands of thugs and terrorists

Rather than requiring our government employees, police, judges, and lawyers to employ some common sense…
* there is a massively expensive drug bureaucracy
* the street price of drugs is artificially high
* the cartels are fabulously wealthy and consequently vicious
* the cartels love us for our accommodating drug laws
* the cartels can afford to corrupt governments
* the cartels can afford weapons and their own troops
* drug dealers commit crimes to protect their business
* drug users commit crimes to support their habits
* drug usage goes on virtually unabated as new sellers and buyers step into every brief vacuum that is created by incarceration
* more people are suffering from our pathetically ignorant drug policy then there would be if drugs were legalized, and far more than if it were also, controlled

As for marijuana, its immediate decriminalization should be a viable initiative because it would…
* offer cancer patients some easy to obtain relief from their pain
* free up the jails that are housing the thousands of non-violent inmates

* take the much of the profit out of drugs for the criminal elements that are the producers and dealers
* allow a tidy increase in states tax revenue from the product's sale

The downside could be increased usage… or maybe not. And we would almost certainly have to regulate this product in the same manner that we do with alcohol and the public use of cigarettes. Then the tax revenue and the incumbent savings derived from not over taxing our jail system would offset this marginal expense many times over.

Of course, there would be the hordes of DEA employees and related government worker bees who would have to find legitimate work for themselves. But is that worse than the current situation? The drug problem is not So, much a problem with drugs, which of course it is to a degree, but is a substantially greater problem to abate because of the vast number of government employees and others who make a tidy living off of it.

In 2012 with a reversal of policy, the federal prosecutors, who may have thought that they felt obligated to do something about the reasonable access marijuana, decided to launch a crackdown on the pot dispensaries in California. The owners were threatened with criminal charges and confiscation of property even though their businesses have been legal for years in the state. They were given 45 days to "get out of Dodge". That change of attitude followed a two-year period of intentionally relaxed enforcement by the feds. So, how did we go from some compassion for the very ill, to none at all? What suddenly got into their illogical heads? Did they feel the need to justify their immense bureaucracy that was under worked? Probably!

Note: Our war on drugs is an unacceptable substitute for common sense.

Apparently however, that thought process is in short supply when it comes to the profiteers, bunglers and self-righteous morons who are employed in government. So, again, what is it with all of those worker bees who are supposed to be in "service" to this country, and have this mindless preoccupation with minding other's business? And that just aint-a-happenin' folks.

Afghanistan Again-istan

In the past the US had encounter serious problems relating to the reestablishment of the Taliban in Afghanistan. Their planting of poppies provides much of the revenue that is used to support the insurgencies in Iraq, Pakistan, Afghanistan and elsewhere. At one point our government invited a cooperating War Lord to the US for an information verbal exchange about the war. Then after pumping him for his firsthand details of the drug trade, the DEA arrest him. This unbelievable action was directed toward a person who took a major risk to volunteer his assistance in our war effort. Yep, we jailed him!

The unmistakable message to others who might wish to cooperate with the US was clear. We can't be trusted to act rationally as long as our policies are impaired by zealots that are masquerading as public servants. Could that somehow be what the intent of the incarceration was? Was there any other train of thought involved?

We spend hundreds of millions of dollars in a failed and fruitless effort to eradicate the poppy growing fields, only to alienate the poorest of farmers whose livelihood relies on this crop. Then those endeavors drove them into the camps of the Taliban and raised the price of heroine, which in turn increases their wealth and power. Will we ever learn how counterproductive this war on drugs is? Isn't anyone willing to prevent this mindless waste of lives and resources? Can the access to drugs be any worse that the slaughter of thousands of people that is in some way due to our policies?

The government could not have created a worse scenario for the US if they had put its minds to it, between the drug trade, the price of oil, becoming the target of radicals, and the loss of world prestige.

Ruling by Religion

This brings me to an important, under-acknowledged point about politics. There is a contingent in America who would prefer to punish certain behaviors rather that understand and deal with them in a responsible manner. Among them are conservatives who are on the loose-morals warpath, and who are contemptuous of our natural excitement with various gratifications. They do their best to influence government policies in the direction of their insensitive mindset.

If we could truly separate church and state in this country we would be far better off for it. But because of religion's pervasive influence in society, we turn a blind eye to its negative and accommodating role in our problems. Perhaps this is because we believe that no harm can be done if the intention being promoted is deemed proper. But one man's responsible is another man's oppression. So, have you gotten the idea that some of America's problems, both internally and externally, are the result of these influences? If not, you may be a contributor to the difficulties.

True believers can't help trying to inflict their personal values on others, So, I have to ask…
* Is it really anyone's business, besides the mothers, whether an abortion is performed or not?
* Is being gay or having sex outside of marriage really a sin that needs to be curbed by church or civil law?
* Are the alleged family values actually important values or are they simply the crusader's values?
* Does having legal, same-sex partnerships harm anyone?
* Should any of the church's persuasions, whether noble or not, be encouraged by government?
* Do we need to have In God We Trust and Under God promoted on our currency or in the Pledge of Allegiance?

On this last question…
* What exactly is the benefit of repeating this pledge in schools or in public meetings in the first place?
* Does repeating it mindlessly do anything to enhance ourselves or the country?
* Who are we trying to impress with this declaration of loyalty anyway?
* As long as we are not working against America, is patriotism anyone else's business but our own?
* If it makes some people feel good, do we all need to follow in lockstep with others like sheep?

Prostitution's Bad Rap

Let's make one thing perfectly clear at the outset. Prostitution is only a crime against the repressive attitudes that have been promulgated by the churches in this country and have consequently been supported by our government. It is not a crime against people except in the eyes of those who have been indoctrinated with this repressive mentality since their youth.

The right-wing thinkers in the US are continually on the war path against sexual freedom and gratification because they have been told forever that it is a sin to have sex occur outside of marriage, and that it is supposed to be utilized only for the procreation of children. So, those who do not want to have children are supposed to do exactly what? Abstain? Because there are So, many in this vocal, anti sex group, laws have arisen to punish those who step outside of their mindset.

Prostitution has been designated and vilified as the first occupation, and it has been a fact of life since long before recorded history. This status alone is quite an achievement for something So, evil. The religious right will contend that this profession is not victimless, but they rarely put up logical, factual arguments against it that are not a direct repercussion of it being illegal. That is not to say that they may not have thoughtful arguments. They do, however, tend to revolve obliquely around those antisocial behaviors that may occur due to repression and the creation of nonsense laws.

Sex is similar to an impenetrable balloon. If you press in somewhere, the result is an expansion somewhere else, but the volume remains essentially static. In this same light, prostitution like prohibited drugs, is never going to go away, and we might as Well, deal with that fact in a reasonable, responsible manner. The current dogma about both of these subjects is clearly not working.

Societies through history have had more sensible attitudes toward sex than we have in this country. They find it prudent to indulge in a certain amount of pragmatism. If you can't eradicate a situation, work with it… something we should consider.

One problem is, of course, that there can be sexually transmitted diseases (STDs) derived from casual sex. But in this country, rather than have effective solutions, we prefer to listen to those who have been dominated by preachers who have managed to get into their collective ears. Sex is not inherently evil regardless of how many profess it to be so, or how vehemently the chorus of voices asserts that it is. It is simply natural.

Some other countries and areas within the US have taken steps to regulate this activity by relegating it to specific sex zones and then mandating regular medical examinations. This is a far cry from the popular US stance of having sex police patrol known solicitation areas and make arrests for something that is none of their business.

If I could make just one observation about the church-inspired mentality toward sex it would be that these people just can't mind their own damn business. They need to get with the no-harm/no-foul perspective, rather than wasting the taxpayer's money.

In one way of thinking, dating can be thought of as a form of prostitution. It uses the money incentive (dinner and a movie, perhaps) with the exchange of sexual favors as reciprocity. So, when this activity is with people who *may* be more than casually interested in each other, the arguments against their behavior fade into the background. The real problem seems to be with the exchange of currency by those people who seldom know each other and may not meet again. I suggest that this is not too far distant from the more socially acceptable bar pick-up scene.

As for prostitution not being victimless, victims are created by the very laws that are meant, I suppose to protect us. No one denies that children and young adults can be harmed by imposed sex, and that they must be protected against this. On the other hand, only a fool would deny that aberrant sexual behaviors are frequently a function of state mandated repression. Take away the free expression of this activity and our innate programming can go a bit haywire. And it is not just the state that restricts our sexual freedom. Attitudes derived from religion are playing a big hand in that process as well.

Like the war on drugs, the war on sex has a similar result and influence on society, such as corruption and violence. Prostitution is pushed into the back alleys and is controlled by those with a money incentive. Remove the third-party money thing by legalizing this service and that nefarious incentive goes away. But this will take a serious rethinking of the subject, in association with a rebuke of the sanctimonious folks who think that this is somehow their business. Sexual attitudes ebb and flow over long periods of time, So, I don't see the majority coming to new conclusions anytime soon.

One study concluded that the laws we enforce against the sex trade cost everyone in the US $22 per year in police services. While that may not sound like a lot per individual, the total is spread across some 400 million of us from diapers to grave. And it does not take into consideration the toll on the people involved, which cannot be measured in dollars. So, by my math, sex police cost the US some $880 million and much more per year.

Travel in Excess

There are times when Congresspersons may need to travel in order to see dramatic national events firsthand, like the devastation caused by hurricane Katrina… but not twenty or fifty at a time. Perhaps one or two could make the trip and report their findings back to their colleges. These tripping Congresspersons…
* do speak English, don't they?
* have phones, don't they?
* know how to use email, don't they?

Then there are the politicians who accept travel perks from our largest corporations when it suits their fancy. Senate Majority Leader Harry Reid was one of the more egregious offenders in this crowd of easy takers. He had been given, as of a count in 2009, some 40 private (non-government business) jet trips since 2001 at who knows what real cost to the taxpayers. Have you ever been offered one?

Reid's response to the critics was: "I am confident that I have never been influenced by anyone who provides me with the courtesy of a private plane".

What we can glean from his statement is that…
* confidence comes a bit too easily for Reid
* he is not influenced by perks in the same way that ordinary people would be
* courtesy is not another word for bribery
* corporations are just nice folks
…or perhaps he is just an outright liar

Some might choose to believe that Reid was doing his duty to our country while simultaneously being lavished with perquisites, but how can we? The conflict of interest is beyond obvious, although this does not seem to be part of his consciousness. Nor does he demonstrate anything resembling guilt or embarrassment in his remarks about it. How can anyone not feel some measure of disquiet for unethically and aggressively taking advantage of a corrupt environment?

Representative Charles Rangel was another case in point. In spite of being admonished for taking corporate sponsored trips to Antigua and St. Martin, which is a violation of Congressional gift rules, he denied knowledge of their corporate backing. So, let's see. He is either a liar or beyond dumb. Can you spell *liar?*

And of course, Reid and Rangel were not alone with their easy virtue. Nearly all members of Congress are known for taking a vast array of bribes from lobbyists and corporations. In fact, it is so flagrant that many of us have simply turned a blind eye to this corrupt behavior. And amazingly, the graft is being taken without anyone having done anything unethical or illegal, if you believe the Congressional spin-misters. So, how can the rest of us get in on this sweet game?

Bill Creation

No, this is not some guy that you might remember from High School. Rather it is the convoluted, inequitable process by which ideas may be offered up in Congress in the hope of becoming law. At other times these bills act as bargaining chips, such as with: if you support my pork, I'll support yours. It does not matter much if the other guy's bills are good, bad, or ugly in this vote swapping scenario.

Occasionally there is no expectation of a bill's passage because the motive behind it is a ploy that is designed to embarrass the opposition when they vote against it. Look to the dead-on-arrival bill to repeal the health care law by Republicans in 2012 as an example of this nonsense.

In an ideal world, bills would be presented to benefit the country or to right some wrong. Far too often, however, they are the creations of those interest groups who were not elected to office but have their Congressperson's ardent attention to further their own agendas. I refer of course to the PACs (Political Action Committees).

It would be helpful here if we understood that a Congressperson's principal, unprincipled, loyalty is not to their constituency but to the afore-mentioned groups who go about distributing their generous campaign funds, gifts, and perks.

These lobbyists are also, the same folks who are occasionally responsible for drafting our legislation (no kidding) when it suits their purposes. More than once a bill has been crafted to regulate the very industry that writes it. In this situation the bill is more watered down than one might expect if it were proposed by an unbiased congressperson.

Having bills that are written by others has become a convenience for our elected officials because they are far too busy dealing with fund raisers to think about the public good for more than a few minutes at a time. Because of this diversion of proper interest, it would not be unreasonable to wonder how much thought actually goes into evaluating the bills that are written by lobbyists. We should also, ask how much of these bills are even understood by those who then offer them up for a Congressional vote.

Now you know how loopholes are created... intentionally.

Bill Suppression

All bills that are written do not necessarily garner a vote in Congress just because they may have been drafted for that purpose. They must first be...
* assigned to the appropriate committee - maybe
* permitted by the committee chairperson to be debated - maybe
* voted out of their committee - maybe
* permitted to come to the floor for a vote - maybe

This means there are a lot of maybes that a bill go through with a succession of good-ol'-boy give and take actions. You give and they take. Or perhaps it is now you owe them one. Then if that labored process goes well the bill's author needs to harvest enough support from his or her peers... more horse-trading. Finally, the happy day might arrive when a vote can be taken... maybe, unless there is a filibuster, or some other procedure invoked that stops the bill dead in its tracks. Aint politics grand?

Congress is what happens when an amoral, unprincipled, body is in charge of making the laws

The Balance of Power

The battle between the Democrats and the Republicans is not unlike the previously advertised competition between Pepsi and Coke for the pocketbooks of cola drinkers. The game was designed to eliminate as much outside competition as possible by ignoring or actively undermining the competing beverage companies.

One would not be faulted for imagining that neither Pepsi nor Coke much care who wins these cola wars because they are both winners as they divide up the spoils between themselves. According to press reports I have seen, they had gone So, far as to prevent competing cola companies from purchasing the prized, lighted-door vending machines.

In a similar way our corporations probably don't care who appears to be in control of government because in the end it is they who are in charge with their influence on both parties. They financially support both sides for a very good reason. Their domination of process is very effective. As a result of this corporate manipulation, politicians have made the term populist candidate virtually disappear from our lexicon. It has been relegated to the political trash heap because it is no longer a productive platform for generating contributions.

Years earlier the term socialism went the same way. This was not So, much because that form of economics was a dreadful idea, but it was because it might have reduced the corporate influence in politics. Power to the people was to be avoided at all costs.

To my way of thinking there are two ways to look at the socialism… equality and justice. In days past, the Russians practiced a form of equality where the under-educated held an inordinate amount of power and made destructive decisions through their centralized government.

The preferred form of socialism is where justice and fair play are used as guidelines for making economic decisions. In this scenario no one holds power or wealth that is disproportionate to their contribution to the whole. Excessive wealth coexisting with gross poverty would be a target of this concept, and one that is regrettably ignored. Why?
Can you guess who holds the power in America? A clue: It's not the needy or under privileged. Just like history being written by the victors, the distribution of wealth is dictated by the wealthy.

When the lack of equitable tax payments by the super-rich eventually became a mild embarrassment to the politicians who voted in their sweetheart loopholes and benefits, a Minimum Alternate Tax was inaugurated. It was deemed that the wealthy should pay some minimum tax to balance out their many benefits and tax loopholes. The result of this fix (don't you just love that word here) is that people with incomes in the millions of dollars can still end up paying a lower tax rate than those with modest incomes.

In 2011 the tax issue came up again when a billionaire stated that his rate was lower than that of his home employees. Obama, sometime thereafter, took up the tax-the-rich battle cry and was immediately met with the counter cry of class-warfare by the Republican leadership. Hard as I try, the only warfare I can detect is the war that is promulgated by the rich who want to keep their wealth. And they offer no apology for their greed. Maybe we do need class warfare in order to correct the gross injustices that prevail in our tax system.

Minimum Wage

I would not care to be categorized as a liberal when it comes to politics in general, but what is it with minimum wage and healthcare in this country? We lost our top socio-economic ranking in the world many years ago, and we are now in the neighborhood of 14th place when compared to other developed countries. This has been an inexcusable downhill trend that can be attributed to declining public educational scores and the years of politicians listening to lobbyists and PACs instead of serving the people.

I remember when the minimum wage was $1.10 per hour. It was barely sufficient for a kid like me working as a stock clerk during summer vacation, and a far cry from being adequate for anyone trying to pay rent and raise a family. Yet not much has changed in the fifty-some years since then. Prior to the most recent increase in the minimum wage there had been more than ten years of fruitless discussions about it in Congress. Well, actually it's been minimal talk and a lot of stonewalling by those who are financially beholding to or are philosophically aligned with business.

It is a shameful reflection on the federal government that there are many states with a higher minimum than the federal rate. Half a dozen states have a higher rate than even the latest, proposed increase, which required more than a year to phase in.

Following in lockstep with every proposed or incorporated minimum wage increase are the business voices who predict that the economy

could falter as a result of a boost in a pathetic pay scale. Their logic goes thusly...
* because of the burden on small businesses, the lowest wage earners may be fired
* product costs will increase
* the poor will suffer doubly

So, the corporate answer to dealing with the poorest on the wage scale spectrum is to let their pitiful pay be further eroded by inflation, as we had done for the last ten years. A case of: I've got mine, you're on your own.

During the last half century there has not been a noticeably adverse repercussion resulting from giving the lowest wage earners a decent break. A few store owners might have had to cut back slightly or temporarily on their business or lifestyles. A few low wage earners may possibly lose their jobs at a handful of marginal businesses. But what is that downside in comparison to a benefit to the millions who scrape by on the pittance that we allow businesses to pay them?

In stark contrast to the above arguments, no one seems to complain about...
* computer programmers, like myself, making $50 to $200 per hour and their adverse effect on the economy

* the lawyers who have created a legal system
that permits them to charge substantially more
than that
* dot.com whizzes that have drained hundreds of
millions or billions of dollars from startup
companies with their immense stock options
* some doctors and dentists who can never make
enough off of people's suffering

Even plumbers, electricians and other
tradespersons may have billing rates that can be
out of proportion to their skill levels. There is no
detectable outrage from the public or a
noticeable drag on the economy from these and
other sectors.

More importantly we do not rein in the drug
companies or fix the broken, for-profit/not-
people oriented healthcare system. But the poor,
Well, that's another story. They are at our mercy,
and we don't have much of that commodity to
expend. We just don't give a damn. And by being
poor they have no power or advocates with
which to turn things around.

Why is it that we are So, willing to penalize this
undereducated, underprivileged class in this
country? In stark contrast, if the corporations
make millions of dollars off of the backs of its
laborers, then So, be it? Would you have a
problem paying an extra 25 cents for a burger in
order to support a higher minimum wage?

This country is run by the wealthy, for the wealthy, with minimal regard for the welfare of the working class that make them rich.

According to my education in business economics, increases in wages will...
* increase demand for more products
* which brings increased production
* which brings increased productivity
* which brings increased hiring
* which quickly mitigates the aforementioned increase in wages

Sounds reasonable, doesn't it? Even if the above logic were not perfectly efficient, the net effect of increasing the minimum wage would be to slightly adjust the distribution of wealth... a little from the rich... some amount to the poor. But still, this minimal concession to the needy is anathema to the wealthy and their wealth promoters in government. They like their money, and they insist on hanging on to as much of it as they can.

Perhaps the best justification for a minimum wage increase comes from our neighbor to the South. Mexico Incorporated is run by a small handful of super-wealthy families (one of whom became the richest in the world in 2010) that feed off of the underclass. The result is that their...

* wealthy remain obscenely rich
* desperately poor run to America
* underpaid police are corrupt
* underpaid government employees are corrupt
* drug cartels are out of control
* bands of armed rebels run amuck because even the risk of death is considered a viable alternative to poverty

Meanwhile, back to all's fair in business at America.com. According to the Wall Street Journal in 2005, 1% of the wealthiest Americans earned 21% of the income while the bottom 50% of the people earned 13%. And there is good reason to believe that this situation has gotten incrementally worse in the subsequent years.

According to Forbes Magazine, the 400 wealthiest people, or about 0.00001% of the population, own 13% of the gross national product, or some $1.5 trillion worth. This is $1.5 million million
 for 400 people! That is probably more money than they could spend in a lifetime if they went on a normal shopping spree 24 hours per day, seven days a week for the rest of their lives.

Even the middle class has come under financial pressure due to years of giveaways to the already rich by an out of touch Congress. Actually, out of touch would be giving the President and those in Congress an I'm-stupid pass that they don't deserve. In reality they are Well, aware that their giveaways to the rich are primarily to themselves and their already Well, healed friends. Every tax cut is shamelessly designed with this elite class in mind and has only a scrap or two to quell the unrest of the real taxpayers.

George Bernard Shaw, author: *"A government which robs Peter to pay Paul can always depend on the support of Paul."*

One of the tragic side effects of disproportionate wages and other economic inequities is that it encourages the proliferation of crime. When people do not have adequate (and we can all debate just what that might mean) opportunities, a significant percentage of them will resort to anti-social behavior out of desperation or in the belief that crime will bring them a better opportunity.

So, rather than providing for a reasonable distribution of wealth in this country, we elect to build more and more jails in which to house the increasing number of miscreants that we have created, never recognizing how much the country is being penalized for its gross stupidity. Oops, I forgot that the rich and powerful are not really impacted by this.

Let me point out that once again that in 2007 the Congress did not ignore its own minimum wage. It raised its base pay to $170.000. And that is before taking into account their second-to-none health benefits plus their retirement plans which kick in after achieving office. Are your health and retirement policies anywhere near this delicious? Do you even have health and retirement plans?

It was reported in 2011 that the average wealth of all members of Congress (based on their mandatory financial discloser forms) had increased 25 percent over the previous year… significantly better than the average American. While no one has come forward to present evidence that their voting records have contributed to this increase, it is hard to imagine that there are not copious bad apples in this barrel.

Minimum Health

Let me relay a statistic that was published in 2009 which appears to be credible. The average US cost (not necessarily out of pocket) for healthcare is over $8100 per person for far less than universal coverage. This results in millions who cannot afford coverage, and millions more who must rely on high deductible plans to have any healthcare at all. Other industrialized nations spend half that amount to cover everyone from birth to death. The reasons for this disparity are several…

* the paranoia about socialized medicine that is whipped up by the doctors and insurance companies
* high prescription costs to US citizens that are indirectly promoted by Congress
* inefficient hospitals and clinics on ego trips that have expensive, redundant equipment
* specialists that are permitted to charge high fees for what sometimes amounts to minimal efforts… have you been to a dermatologist lately?
* and worst of all are the nearly unregulated, *for-profit*, insurance companies that siphon off billions of dollars from the care system

On the last point on the above. Let me emphasize that American healthcare insurance is truly a for-profit system. This means that a significant percentage of your health cost goes to line the pockets of insurance company stockholders and the executives whose salaries and bonuses are based on performance. Their pay, curiously enough, is not related to providing superior care. Rather it is based on how little healthcare they can get away with paying for.

Michael Moore, activist: *"We allow these [insurance] companies to profit off of the sick."*

Our Canadian neighbor to the north has a medical system which appears to work fairly well. Virtually everyone there has healthcare even though they may have to be on a waiting list for some of the procedures. In that case they can fall back on paying for care out of their own pocket, if they choose.

While my experience with this system is limited, I do acknowledge a number of people who have expressed negative attitudes toward Canada's socialized medicine. Perhaps it is a matter of not being able to please all of the people all of the time, perhaps not.

In contrast to the rest of the developed world, our country has the largest percent of personal bankruptcies resulting from people's inability to pay for their high medical costs. In fact, until the housing crisis of 2007, it was estimated that one half of all of the bankruptcies in this country were generated by people who could not afford to pay for these bills. And we have yet to fix that situation.

In Canada and many European countries, virtually no one has had to initiate bankruptcy because of their medical bills. To the contrary, people die in America because they lack rudimentary healthcare. And what do we do about it? Mostly we believe the propaganda about the evils of socialized medicine. Instead of having the best healthcare system in the world we have the worst among the developed countries, and we allow it to remain that way.

The real death panels (a phrase invention by Sarah Palin regarding Obamacare) are to do nothing. A Harvard study found that 39.000 people die per year due to insufficient healthcare or to having none.

Regarding the details of the Canadian healthcare system as I understand it...
* health procedures are rated (weighted) on two criteria... the cost of the procedure and its probability of its success
* high-risk/high-cost procedures get the lowest priority
* low risk/low-cost procedures get the highest priority
* healthcare is allocated based on a procedure with a higher priority before one that has a lower priority
* if you have a poor prognosis and the cost is high, you may not receive benefits paid for by the state
* if you have a good prognosis and the cost is not excessive, your procedure is assured
* in between, the allocation of health services is based on balancing priorities
* if you do not qualify for coverage or immediate coverage you can arrange to pay your own medical bills

The bottom line is that more people are covered in Canada, and the healthcare system is not drained of billions of dollars by insurance companies. In this country perhaps one dollar in three goes toward insurance - money that could be better used to help people with their medical problems.

Even if the Canadian system is not perfect, it is light years ahead of ours where vast numbers of people can't afford healthcare and may be forced to use the bankruptcy card or flood the emergency rooms (which the rest of us end up paying for).

An argument for some who are against socialized medicine is that it is a bureaucracy that decides who may live (gets medical care) and who may die for lack of care. If one ignores the actual mechanics of this system, it sounds scary. And this foolish argument is what many Americans are led to believe.

So, if not everyone can afford full healthcare due to its high costs, there must be some mechanism to manage that shortfall. Our current strategy is to have...
* the highest costs in the world for less than full coverage
* many who cannot afford to make insurance payments

* emergency rooms which are required to care for everyone, including the uninsured, and then pass that bill onto the insured if it is not paid by the patient
* people that die because they cannot afford doctors and medicine
* bankruptcies that result from high health costs

When it comes to the various alternatives for healthcare, there are several different options…
* let people die that have no insurance (do you think this doesn't actually happen?)
* allocate healthcare only to those who can afford it
* have an outrageously expensive, for-profit insurance system that converts billions of our premium dollars into their own pockets
* have those people with the better cost vs. prognosis equation receive the treatment first

My vote is for the last option. It is inherently un-American for a person's income to determine if they can receive treatment? Do we do this with school availability, police services, or fire protection? We might show caring for those who are injured in a natural disaster, but we care little about those in a healthcare disaster.

Another feature of our imperfect healthcare system is that politicians are eager to protect the profits of the drug industry to the point where people have to travel to Mexico or Canada to be able to purchase lower priced drugs… often the same drugs that are available here. Then our Congresspersons pass laws that permit the border guards to confiscate those drugs as a punishment for the desperate people who are trying to save money. So…

* Why are American drugs cheaper in other countries anyway?
* Do we believe that adequate, affordable healthcare should only be available for the middle (maybe) and upper classes?
* Since Congress's healthcare system is unequaled, why should they bother themselves with the rest of us?

Yet another inequitable side to medical care and medical billing is what I will call the two-tier system. This occurs when, if you have insurance, your insurance company pays the doctor a discounted amount of their purposely inflated invoice. The patient then covers the ever-increasing co-payment (remember when it was $5?), which goes to the doctor. (This is the clever method of transferring more of the medical costs to the patient's back and off that of the insurance companies). On the other hand, if you cannot afford an insurance plan, you pay the full, inflated price. So, those who least can afford health insurance end up paying the highest price which subsidizes those who are insured. As a result, the poor go without coverage or use the emergency rooms which others pay for.

Health insurance corporations are much like the casinos in Las Vegas. No matter which patients win or lose, they come out on top. There are few situations that might put their bottom line at risk. There is just the continuous inflow of money (drained from your healthcare) while the rest of us are trying to manage their escalating invoices.

For each dollar spent on healthcare, a third is siphoned off by insurance companies. Then they tout the virtues of the free market system, all while they are busy bribing elected officials to maintain the status quo. Meanwhile the naïve public pays their enormous medical bills and wonders what can be done… in silence.

In 2010 Goldman Sachs reported that insurance companies are willing to lose individual subscribers or an entire company (due to high premiums) from their roles because they make up for those losses with higher premiums. A smaller pool of clients does not mean lower profits. What is does mean is that they are willing to put their profits above healthcare for the country. For the insurance executives, it's all about their bonuses.

Never be confused about this - insurance companies are in the profit business and absolutely not in the healthcare business.

Minimum Medicare

Another potential tragedy in the offing with healthcare is Medicare. Because the government is run by the members of the already-rich-and-got-great-coverage club, there is little concern for those who are not part of their good ol' boy system. Congress has made earning a living progressively less profitable for doctors who are willing to see Medicare patients. Unless you are in this category you probably didn't know there was a problem brewing. But your time to find out will be coming soon enough.

Now I am not here to defend the income of doctors. They are already sufficiently compensated for their efforts, perhaps not like it used to be; say down from an annual BMW 750i to an Infinity G. But a problem occurs when their billings, which are submitted to Medicare, are paid at a rate of pennies on the (inflated invoice) dollars. As a result of this shortfall in revenue, there is a disincentive toward serving that type of patient. And some of doctors are beginning to deny Medicare-paid treatment to their patients. To put this situation another way, rather than having doctors satisfied with only a portion of their exaggerated bills from Medicare, they may disallow Medicare patient billing and start asking patients to pay their full invoice up front.

Let's say that a doctor might receive $10 from the government for a $100 procedure and $35 from your co-pay. The Medicare-denied scheme means that you could now pay $100 for a visit and then work to receive the $10 from Medicare, making to procedure cost $90, or almost three times as much as an insured individual would pay. This change in billing practice amounts to increased revenue to doctors and a reduction in their government-required paperwork.

If one assumes the inflated medical fee are only used as a bargaining chip against the insurance companies and Medicare, then anyone who has to pay the full amount is being taken to the cleaners. With the government-reduced fees that are paid to Medicare doctors we have the following…
* medical societies allow the inflated bills to both Medicare and insurance companies because they know that they will be heavily discounted
* people without insurance pay the inflated rate because some doctor's insurers will not permit (as if it was any of their business) their covered doctors to offer their non-insured patients a discount (which occurred at what used to be my dentist's office)
* because the government wastes billions of dollars on pork projects, on too many bureaucrats, pointless drug interdiction, and a losing war, they have to cut back elsewhere, like with services to the public

* Medicare patients who cannot find willing doctors will have to foot their own bills or go without, which is an unacceptable scenario
* in the worst-case scenario, Medicare patients may have to cover 80 percent of their inflated bills if they cannot locate a cooperating doctor who is willing to see them

Let me go back to the insurance company's requirement that doctors not discount their services to the uninsured. The reasons behind this policy are to...
* obscure the discounted amount of doctor's invoices that they reimburse
* prevent doctors from being in competition with the insurance companies for receiving dollars from patients
* make sure that as much revenue flows through the insurance system as possible to increase their profits, and by forcing people to buy insurance

One doctor's office which stopped servicing Medicare covered patients and many other insurance companies, reduced their fees to correspond more closely to the income they would likely receive from third party billings. So, instead of charging $150 for a procedure to get back perhaps $15 in insurance payments, plus a $35 co-pay, they began charging the patients $50 directly. And with that change they do away with the expensive submission of paperwork to either the insurance companies or government or both.

Many Americans are naively happy that there are health insurance companies to help them through medically tough times without understanding how costly that service really is. They might not be So, pleased in knowing that the insurance companies are responsible for creating the artificially high medical costs while siphoning off billions of dollars from healthcare to support...
* a huge insurance infrastructure
* inflated executive salaries
* extravagant bonuses
* stockholder dividends because they are public corporations

More and more doctors are being forced to either retire early from what is becoming an increasingly less economical practice, or to drop insurance covered patients to maintain their income.

You might care to know that some CEOs of insurance companies are making bonuses in the tens of millions of dollars per year for their technical skills at reducing your healthcare reimbursements. Oh yes, they do make their multi-million-dollar salaries on top of this as well.
The bonuses that they receive are because these folks have become adept at squeezing the doctors and patients alike.

To pin it down, the problem with healthcare in this country is that…

* people pay obscenely high health insurance premiums for less than full coverage
* doctors get pennies on the dollar for their inflated billings to insurance companies and the government
* patient co-payments have steadily increased in order to pay off the doctors for their lower reimbursement
* the government and insurance companies pretend that they are doing the consumers a favor
* our corrupted leaders repeat the chant that socialized medicine is bad for America
* advocates for socialized medicine have to defend their position against the lies emanating from the insurance industry. Guess who has the most money to spend on that debate.

The insurance companies have an incentive to reduce or deny medical coverage whenever possible because it directly affects their bottom line, which has nothing to do with providing superior health care. What seems totally arrogant and incomprehensible is that these companies occasionally will not disclose whether they will cover a particular procedure in advance of a person having that procedure. What? People are left to guess as to the affordability of going ahead with their medical care. Can you spell deterrent?

One solution for people without an insurance plan might be to purchase only catastrophic healthcare coverage. Then locate a doctor who will discount their rates for uninsured visits. This would result in an outlay that is more than the typical co-pay, but the cost of insurance coverage would be far less. Finding a cooperative doctor or dentist may be difficult though. I have been turned down several times with this request but managed to find a cooperating dentist. Apparently some doctors like their higher revenue from the uninsured patients, and care little for these people's financial welfare.

Now it is not just lawyers that we have a good reason to dislike.

Another option would be to find a company that acts like a brokerage by bargaining with doctors for uninsured rates that are comparable to co-pays plus receipts from insurance submissions. What does this say about a medical profession that forces people to think about using a broker?

Illegal Immigration

Conspiracy can be defined as a planned or executed illegal activity between two or more persons. It can also, be said about politicians and big business when they pretend to be doing something about aliens in order to placate US citizens. Depending on whom you ask, we either do or don't have a problem.

The <u>do</u> side seems to suggest that illegal immigrants…
* are involved in a disproportional amount of criminal activity
* raise the cost of emergency room fees for all because they do not have healthcare, and do not pay when utilizing this service
* require us to spend millions of dollars on border control
* use our schools, roads, and other services without paying for the infrastructure
* may not pay income taxes

The *don't* side seems to suggest that illegal immigrants…
* will take many of the jobs that Americans won't
* are a cheap, plentiful, and reliable source of manual labor
* insure that the crops will be picked

The Heritage Foundation, a conservative think tank, has estimated that the lifetime cost of illegal immigration to the government at $22.000 per legal resident because of…
* under payment of all taxes
* additional school costs for their larger families
* unearned income credits
* driving without insurance

* education in Spanish
* expanded jail populations
* social security benefits

So, it turns out that our cheap tomatoes are not really so cheap after all. They are being subsidized by diverting their true costs into other sectors of the economy. Even if the need for cheap labor were a legitimate reason for permissive border control, the real cost of permitting a flood of aliens may be too high to justify.

Need evidence that the government is talking a good game rather that playing one? Consider our research facility at Area 51 in the Nevada desert. There are no fences at this top-secret location, just electronic devices that detect anything larger than a mosquito. Nothing gets past their blockade undetected. This implies that we have the technology but not the interest to stop the influx of illegal aliens cold.

FYI: The infamous Area 51 is a money maker for those with a vivid imagination. There have been TV specials for years on this subject. Does anyone really believe that a life form could travel here at the speed of light (impossible) for 26 years from the nearest star system? An interesting aspect about speed is that the mass of an object increases exponentially with its speed. The mass of this object would reach infinitively (impossible) as it approached anywhere near the speed of light. So, a 26-year trip would likely take 260 years or more even if it was able to gather propulsion enough energy from nearly empty space to complete a trip.

Getting back to the prior subject… Perhaps we do not want to offend Mexico by reducing the US dollars that are sent back by undocumented workers. One theory about this is that the dollars sent to Mexico do not always chase American products and therefore act to keep a lid on inflation as our currency becomes their de facto currency. In other words, if we can print and use US dollars that end up mainly as the currency in a foreign country, we have essentially gotten goods for nothing. It would be akin to our taking out a personal loan and then having to pay back only a portion of it.

Having a guest worker program may be an unenforceable plan that some are contemplating. If we permit aliens to enter with this type of visa, what will prevent them from staying permanently? We don't adequately monitor the foreign students or temporary visas holders (potential terrorists) now as it is. Why should we expect that this might turn out any differently with a work visa? The truth may be that government administrations have known how easily this program would fail. Perhaps they hope that people grow weary of the issue, and big business can retain its stoop labor pool.

Immigration Reform

In 2010 Arizona passed the landmark immigration bill 1070 that made headlines around the world. In response the Obama Justice Department sued the state in an attempt to overturn the law. In 2011 Arizona countersued the feds to…
* enforce existing laws
* build more border fences
* provide more border agents
* offer improved technology
* reimburse Arizona for of the costs associated with the jailing of illegal immigrants who are convicted of state crimes

So, what was the response from the Department of Homeland Security? Their spokesperson said…
* "The countersuit had no merit." (Without offering any supporting reasons for that statement)
* "Border staffing is higher than ever." (How much higher than what?)
* "Actions like this ignore all of the statistical evidence." (Which was also, not provided)
* "[It] belittles the significant progress that our men and women in uniform (a little flag waving here) have made." (no examples again)

As I read the fed's argument I could not help but be impressed by the lack of any substantive information. Just blather designed to influence the easily influenced. And this is from the department that was headed by a former Governor of Arizona. It is another example of how easily government department heads obediently follow the prevailing political line.

Just Price Fixing

One out of many examples of how big business controls the government involved the Alcohol Control Board in California a number of years back. Because the state's liquor distributors wanted to maximize their profits, they lobbied the legislature to set minimum fair-trade prices on beer, wine and alcohol. Let's see… lobbying, PAC money, new laws, yep they all go together. Then the state agency went on to claim that this [legalized price fixing] was designed to help the mom-and-pop stores compete with the big guys. Haven't we been fed these bogus stories regarding mom-and-pop businesses before, like with farmers and crops? Are convenience stores really in danger of going under because of giant supermarkets?

As a result of that beverage law there was no competition allowed by price among any businesses that sold alcohol in California. That is until a mom and pop (whoda thunk) liquor store owner decided to fight city hall. The owner began by offering discount pricing, was threatened, fined, and sued by the state, but eventually prevailed in the courts. Chalk up one for the consumer, and for mom and pop who do not want government or big business interference in their businesses.

Insider Trading Too

In recent years the Securities and Exchange Commission (SEC) has become more active in prosecuting insider trading on the various exchanges. But it has also, had to ignore a gaping failure in their jailing outrageous cheaters.

Members of Congress have given themselves blanket immunity when it comes to (among their other unethical behaviors) using inside information derived from conversations with corporate executives and in other venues. As a result, some members have made millions of dollars from trades that would have landed you or I in jail. And they had shown no interest in cracking down on their own nefarious activities.

Just one more example of why these self-serving public servants will spend massive sums of money (sometimes their own) and copious hours of campaign time to secure a seat in Congress and to richly reward themselves down the road. Then in 2012 after an exposé segment on 60 minutes, Congress did agree to abolish the practice. However, with 99 bottles of beer on the wall - when one of them falls there are still 98 bottles of beer on the wall.

The Eric Holder Affair

In 2012 the NRA lobbied Congresspersons from both parties tried to hold Attorney General Eric Holder in Contempt of Congress. Their participation in this was prompted by their fear that *not* penalizing him for a failure to release documents about gunwalking to smugglers would result in future legislation restricting gun sales.

After months of procrastination, diversion, and finally a refusal to turn over the subpoenaed documents to Congress regarding the guns given to Mexican terrorists (the So, called Fast and Furious caper), the House voted to issue a Contempt of Congress citation to Holder. He was the first Executive Branch member to ever be sighted for criminal contempt. His refusal to provide the requested documentation was claimed to be justified owing to the support of Obama when he proclaimed Executive Privilege (EP) over the matter.

Since Congress is not a judicial body, the contempt citation had to be forwarded to the Justice Department (JD) in Washington DC for prosecution. Well, any damn fool can guess what came next. Deputy Attorney General James Cole issued a statement that the JD would not pursue the indictment of Holder based on the President's claim of EP. He went on to affirm that therefore no criminal act had been committed. The Deputy then went So, far as to articulate that their decision follows a long-standing practice across the administrations of both parties. The only option that was left up to Congress was to issue a civil contempt citation, which does not go through the JD. Case closed.

In 2014 Holder announced his retirement after six years on the job without an objection from the President. There was, of course, the usual choir of well-wishers (Democrats) with praising statements. The White House spokesman said: "He confronted a large number of issues - many of them very complicated." This is doublespeak for not doing a great job. Among the not-so-good performances was a failure to prosecute financial corruption effectively. And for this he will receive a nice pension and perhaps even a lucrative job offer in the financial community.

Corporate Coziness

If anyone is inclined to dispute the unhealthy relationships that take place between business and government they need look no further than a recent scandal at the Federal Aviation Agency (FAA) as prima facie evidence. According to the two whistleblowers who testified before Congress, the agency has routinely pressured its inspectors to ignore and soft pedal safety issues at the airlines. They testified that the FAA is cozy with airline executives, and that their managers have put those personal relationships above the welfare of the flying public.

So, we should ask the obvious question. Don't any of these dodos have to fly on scheduled airlines? Assuming that they do, why would they be inclined to put their own and their family's lives in jeopardy for a short-term friendship? Once again it is our genetic-emotional disposition to ignore potential problems and assume that all will take care of itself. Or in this case, it could be a darker picture of their being Well, compensated for looking the other way.

Note: Whistleblowers would not be needed in government or business if there were not corrupt practices ongoing.

We all know that the government's regulating agencies are supposed to protect us from the malpractices of industries and businesses. While this is very nice in theory, it is often short on execution. One example of the corrupting, open door policy between business and government involved two executives at the National Highway Traffic Safety Administration (NHTSA). These two were subsequently hired by Toyota after having been implicated in the agencies grossly insufficient oversight of that same company.

Does it come as a surprise to anyone that the problems Toyota had with unintended acceleration, inability to brake, and inability to stop the engine were downplayed by the agency? Toyota was So, proud of negotiating their liability to minimal fixes that they triumphantly (and don't you think a bit foolishly) posted those results in a newsletter.

It appears that the two officials referred to above knew that they had an opportunity for a lucrative position with the company that they regulated, and they did not want to upset that applecart. One can only speculate at how often this breach of ethics takes place at our government oversight agencies.

More instances of how business runs our government revolve around safety issues with the toxin BPA that is found in plastics used by the food industry. There have been over 100 studies from government scientists and university laboratories raising health concerns about this compound. So, what was the response of the Food and Drug Administration (FDA)? They pronounced that these plastics are not harmful in the quantities that people would likely encounter them. Then they admitted that in 2008 they relied on just two research studies which were funded by the plastics industry and backed by the American Plastics Council. This might not be as problematical if it were not for the ignored findings of independent researchers. BPA ingestion has been linked to breast and prostate cancer, behavioral disorders, and potential reproductive problems in lab animals.

Because they had such a good example set for them, the plastic's industry is using the same model that the tobacco industry used So, successfully for years…. fight the science, postpone regulation and compensation. Ultimately the science against BPA may become overwhelming, but in the meantime the sales of these plastic products go on unabated. It's all about our genetic-emotional genes because we do not personally know the victims.

During an exposure of government graft, it came to light in 2008 that personnel at the Minerals Management Service (MMS) were enriching themselves by taking bribes from the industry that they are assigned to oversee. Not to give too much print to BP, but the infamous oil spill came about thanks in great part to the cozy factor between the regulators and regulated. BP allegedly had been permitted to violate numerous safety regulations which directly resulted in the loss of the drilling platform, eleven dead workers, and hundreds of millions of gallons of crude spewed into the Gulf of Mexico.

Shortly thereafter, a senior member of the MMS retired, presumably to avoid testifying about his participation. So, as it often turn out in government, white collar criminals frequently get off the hook. It's unlikely that anyone will be charged in the worker's deaths despite the need to hold BP and MMS people responsible for this horrific and preventable deed.

Should we require further proof of the incest has been rampant between the government and business, one has only to look at the statistics coming out about the oil industry regulators. In 2011 it was reported that one out of five employees involved in regulating this industry had been released from some duties because they may come in contact with family members at those industries.

Further, since mid-2008 ten people who were hired as regulators were bared for two years from working where they would come into contact with former employers. With the Bureau of Ocean Energy Management (BOEM), 35 percent of its inspectors have been disqualified because a friend or relative works for a company that they would interact with. Prior to a policy change that was enacted to identify potential conflicts of interest, coziness between the regulators and the regulated went on virtually unchecked.

Rampant Leniency
Government agencies that have the power to fine companies and pursue court actions have

frequently turned into mister nice guy. How often have your heard that the defendants neither admit nor deny wrongdoing when a case is settled? This is undoubtedly the feds way of speeding up the trial process. But is it right? Is this really punishment?

Going hand and hand with this easygoingness are the pennies on the dollar that have been exacted in of court settlements. In the case of the Securities and Exchange Commission (SEC) v Citigroup Inc., losses of more than $700.000.000 to investors had a proposed settlement of just $285.000. To his credit, the US District judge denounced and rejected the SEC's agreement as pocket change when compared to the losses that were incurred. Citicorp had been accused of selling slices of a Class V deal to investors in 2007 without disclosing that they were concurrently betting against half of the assets that were in the deal.

As mentioned earlier, in 2012 the Congress got around to passing an insider trading act specifically targeting trades based on the inside knowledge that Congresspersons pick up on the job. This was a bill that had languished for six years with virtually no support. When a TV expose and a couple of WSJ articles brought this matter to the public's attention during Presidential campaigning, the attitude in Congress changed.

The point I would demonstrate here is with the public statements that two politicians made about it. They said that this law will help restore public trust. I guess these deep thinkers are living in la la land, not recognizing or acknowledging the myriad of other areas where their body's integrity is sorely lacking. That particular band-aid is a non-fix for a larger, gaping wound.

More Good ol' Boys

Political appointments are a necessary evil of our government. There are positions to fill, and someone has to do that job. The general public clearly has insufficient knowledge of who is qualified and who is not, as witnessed by the candidates that they elect to office. On the other hand, the President and his kiss-up-to-keep-my-job advisors are in only a slightly better position to make these judgments. As a result, those who offer up loyalty, money, or favors to advance an administration are likely to benefit from their 'unselfish' service. Of course, this is not limited to the top levels of government. Rather it is endemic to government in general.

We have gotten So, used to having politicians working for themselves that we may ignore their questionable campaign financing and overspending proclivities. Congress, as one example, has passed legislation funding the lavish funerals of our Presidents without asking anyone's permission but themselves. Certainly, they did not ask those of us who end up with the bill. Weren't these now deceased politicians paid more than enough to bury themselves, So, to speak?

In addition to the generous funerals, there is the substantial cost of...
* military bands
* rifle corps
* dozens of funeral cars
* jets flying overhead
* thousands of flowers
* meals and lodging for the invited guests (did you get your invitation?)

Then we have to pay to fly the departed and their entourage to a final resting place on multiple Air Force 747s. Don't you wish you were part of this fraternity that treats itself So, nicely on someone else's dime? No wonder that Betty Ford was overheard to whisper "It's beautiful" at Jerry's funeral, as if she had some right to that extravaganza for which she did not offer to pay one red cent.

Will you get a decommissioned Air Force One, as Regan did near his Presidential library? While President's Ford, Regan, and Kennedy funerals were grand productions, who are the benefactors of this showiness? You? I? It is the politicians who may gain a degree of undeserved credibility from the it rubs off on me effect of these extravaganzas. If we elevate our Presidents to this monarch-like status, then with innocent-by-association we also, tend to elevate Congresspersons as a group. Perhaps there is some small benefit to those who are obsessed with the rich and famous.

We should be aware that our leaders have not been, for the most part, particularly virtuous people since it is not even remotely possible in the world of politics. We should not behave as if they were saints after their deaths because that demonstrates how little attention we pay to their performances during life. This adulation also, tells the politicians that what they are doing in office is ok, which is surely not the case.

Part of keeping Presidential images from being as tarnished as their behavior often dictates resides with the incestuous association they enjoy with the press. The press is about as untainted as are the drug companies that offer perks to the doctors in exchange for their script business. Reporters attending a White House sponsored press event demonstrate their willingness to indulge in a conflict of interest and discount their responsibility to the public. Then who do we have to complain to… the press?

My criticism of our Presidents is not meant to demean all of those who have held that high position, whether they were bumbling, adequate, or enlightened. It is only meant to put their performance into some perspective. They and the millions of government workers run the largest company in the world and are certainly due some respect for that effort. What they are not entitled to is…

* our mostly thoughtless support
* their overly generous benefits
* our tendency to treat Presidents like royalty
* an average of $7.000/year more than we pay for similar work in the private sector

Unjustified respect for people imbues more power on the powerful, makes possible more wealth for the wealthy, and bestows more privilege on the privileged. Is that what we want?

Ethics Free Zone

What we have in government is a runaway corruption train with the engineer (the public) sound asleep. Politicians have learned that there will be virtually no downside to manipulating the system to suit their personal agenda, which is reelection of course, and that they can do So, with near abandon.

Their actions are not the type of graft that one is usually imprisoned for. Rather it is the solicitation of bribery from powerful interests. Office holders know that the clandestine activities of government are largely conducted behind closed doors where the public cannot exercise scrutiny, and *that* convenience makes them nearly invisible and invulnerable to observation by their constituents.

Their only fear might be that an opposition candidate with little to lose may disclose…
* some dark secrets about their behaviors
* what they voted for and against
* who they are in bed with, both politically and personally
…and this dearth of ethics does not apply just to elected officials, but to appointed officials and corporate executives as well.

During the financial meltdown that was promulgated by the home mortgage derivatives scandal, the bailed-out bankers nicely gave themselves a total of $1.6 billion in bonus pay. After an uproar from the public (while Congress did nothing) a czar was appointed to look into this excessive pay scandal. In 2010 after months of diligent study, lawyer and watchdog (not) Kenneth Feinberg came to the mind-boggling conclusion that the corrupt thieves would get to keep all of their ill-gotten pay gains. His logic was that their public shame was sufficient punishment for their misdeeds. Hmmm…
* Do we even know the names of these allegedly shamed individuals?
* Were they shamed enough to return any of the money?

* Where did we get this moron Feinberg from anyway? Could it possibly have been from Wall Street?
* How could this ludicrous decision have been made without some form of quid-pro-quo?

At the end of 2011 the major banks that were part of the melt-down scheme have yet to see even one of their chief executives indicted for fraud. While there is enough of that to go around, these executives appear to be off limits. And this is years after the bubble burst, So, it cannot be a lack of time to gather the incriminating evidence. One might ask: what should we glean from this about what the SEC's job might be? Is it to punish or to protect offenders?

Government Incorporated

Not too many years back the US government employed only one person for every 100 civilians employed by business. That number is now up to sixteen and climbing. Before long we will be in the same numerical boat with Greece, and you know how Well, they are doing, needing a huge bailout in 2012 to remain afloat.

Our national debt is being ignored by those very people who have the most control over it. And why, you should ask, is this happening? Well, in a word it is reelection. They spend the taxpayer's money in massive amounts to placate business and line their pockets. Unfortunately, their constituents do not get the connection between US debt and political corruption. While many of us do not ordinarily label Congresspersons as corrupt. I challenge you to come up with a better explanation for this behavior.

Fixing the Problem

Why is politics broken? There may be hundreds of reasons but here are a few that you may concur with…

* people are innately self-centered
* politicians, with minimal scrutiny of their activities are at the apex of that behavior
* we have been told forever that the two-party system is preferable to having third-party candidates and possible run-off elections, which conveniently limits the options of voters (would you be ok with only 2 telephone companies, or 2 television networks, or 2 banks?)
* politicians apparently find some sadistic gratification in their artificial confrontations with the opposition party
* campaign funding is more productive when the lobbyist are occasionally manipulated by politicians (surprise)
* politicians have discovered that stating their positions can be counter-productive to fund raising
* incumbent politicians, with their established money sources and power bases, stand a far

better chance of winning the next election
because name recognition trumps performance
* since getting reelected is the politician's prime
directive, the majority of their time, directly or
indirectly, is expended in that pursuit, and is not
often used to produce productive legislation
* getting along in the legislature means becoming
subservient to the power brokers who dole out
positions, perks, and penalties
* legislation is accomplished more by who one
will return a favor to, as by the merits of a bill
* there appears to be a fear of Presidential power
and a reluctance to go up against it
* there are no term limits to prevent the
accumulation of power

When Nebraska joined the Union it sought to
resolve a problem of wasted political energy by
instituting a Unicameral legislature. The
members are selected in nonpartisan elections
rather than in partisan primaries. The top two
vote-getters are then entitled to run in the
general election.

Because there are no mandatory party alignments
in the legislature, coalitions tend to address issues
based on a member's philosophy of government,
geographic background, and constituency.
However, almost all the members of the
legislature are affiliated with either the
Democratic or Republican Party, and both
parties explicitly endorse candidates for

legislative seats. But because candidates have to run on their positions rather than party connection, there is less influence peddling by those of longer tenure.

While this and every other system of government is not fool proof, it could be a step in the right direction for the rest of the states. The problem is, of course, that there is an immense amount of inertia in the States and in Congress. Plus, there is a heavy investment in the broken system that we are straddled with. No incumbent politician wants to give up their advantage at reelection. And there are no practical measures available for us to redress the deficiencies.

Government straddles the line between self-serving the politicians and serving the public… leaning heavily toward the politician side.

On Being American

In 2009 my wife and I attended a Smothers Brothers concert. Because I liked them in the late 60's when they had a television show, I was very familiar with their ability to be irreverent toward government, war, and religion. Their show was toned down a bit compared to their TV appearances, but it did have a skit about the Presidents that went something like…
* Washington could not tell a lie
* Nixon could not tell the truth
* Clinton could not tell the difference

* Bush could not tell anything

On leaving the theater I overheard an older couple who were annoyed that the Smothers Brothers would bring politics into their concert…
* Did they think that their show was just about singing?
* Where were these two pinheads when the brothers were doing these routines on TV and stage for a living?
* Might they have agreed with the brother's previous censorship by CBS? (Nixon is reputed to have pressured CBS into firing them)

The point for me was that these two questioned someone's right to present political humor as if it was unclean or un-American. I imagine that those two don't have a clue about the corruption that goes on in government, and that they blindly support the clowns who get elected to office.

Being an American should mean that we do what is best for the country, and that does not mean being silent in the face of deceit and corruption. Short of working for an enemy, no one should be thought of as being un-American because of a stand against incompetence and corruption in Congress or elsewhere.

HOW BUSINESS FAILS US

What You Need to Know
About Business Corruption

TABLE OF CONTENTS

Oversight Reduction
White Collar Crime
White Collar Stupid
Undeserved Credit
Deserved Discredit
Invasion of Privacy
Invasion By Software

What Were They Thinkin'?

Power is not inherently evil, or is it? Ordinary people who have great power visited upon them through their efforts or happy convenience may become changed for the worse. They are no longer ordinary to themselves. Their inner voice tells them that the rules which other have to live by no longer apply, if breaking them is done with stealth. The devil on one shoulder speaks to them more forcefully than the angel on the other.

People in positions of power may revert to their childhood behavior of wanting to have all of the toys, to the point where they will do virtually anything to get them. Having *some* is never quite as fulfilling as having *more*. Multiple, expensive objects can be the objective of an intense desire, and the examples of this behavior are too numerous to mention. This need, far too often, leads to unethical, immoral, or criminal activities in their business dealings. One might think that the number of these miscreants that end up being exposed or land in jail would act as a deterrent to others with insatiable desires. But that appears not to be the case. Apparently great power, like some drugs, dulls the wit.

Fleecing the public should not have to remain a secret for long if we are paying attention to overt manifestations of wealth. One possible conclusion about this lack of exposure is that others who are also, at the top of this game are playing in the same ballpark. Perhaps they are keeping their own secrets and respecting those of their peers. Rats do not rat in other rats.

Voting for any candidate is an essentially a futile exercise, and it denies the truth of corporate manipulation, regardless of which party is elected.

They Auto Do Better

What may be one of the more pathetic businesses in America has been the auto industry. At one time there were a half dozen thriving manufacturers, and that is now down to three. They have gone from producing virtually all US vehicles to producing only a fraction of them. In 2011 GM and Ford's share of the market was less than 20% each.

It's not as if this sorry condition beset the industry overnight. The downhill slide took some fifty years of arrogance to accomplish. That means fifty years of not minding the store while the executives were drawing fancy salaries and bonuses.

How did the industry let this tragedy occur? There are several factors that took place over time…
* several smaller (that are now out of business) manufacturers thought that they could get away with building poor quality cars just because the Big Three did
* when times were good and there was not yet competition from Japan, the manufacturers gave away massive future profits to the unions by granting excessive benefits packages, on top of good salaries
* the sales model for Detroit was to build bigger clunkers, even while automobile demand was inexorably changing toward higher quality and greater fuel efficiency
* billions of advertising dollars were spent (wasted) on marketing to the diminishing number of Americans who still believed in Detroit's bigger is better line of thinking
* lobbying congress to keep the automobile mileage requirements in check in order to permit the greater profit margins on the sale of their oversized slugs
* ignoring the flood of high quality, imported cars until it was too late to mount an effective counterattack, and it may be too late (short of

some miracle) for Detroit to convince us that they do know what is expected and will perform accordingly

Prior to a modest recovery, the government had an opportunity to provide a long-term solution to Detroit's financial problems by...
* temporarily taking over the auto companies with bailout funds and debt repayment provisions
* firing the incompetent top executives and boards of directors
* replacing these people with executives who have demonstrated an ability to manage corporations efficiently
* forcing the unions to make reasonable concessions to limit the blood loss
* insisting on building quality cars that will compete effectively with those coming from abroad

Dumbthink is of course not restricted to automobile companies. In what may be one of the lamest decisions by corporate America, Pfizer Inc. decided to commit more than $87 million toward promoting their previous cash cow, Lipitor. Now this may not seem too outrageous in the high finance world of the drug empire, but this judgment was made after their patent had expired in the fall of 2011. I guess they thought that they could become the Kleenex of this particular segment of prescription drugs. With generic replacements coming onto the market in the future, this was a risky call.

Airline Cattle Call

Let me suggest what might have been a dicey decision adopted by the airline industry… the Airbus 380. You know that huge double decked aircraft that can tote a megaton of people and their luggage halfway across the world without having to refuel. Apparently the developers and the purchasing airlines felt a pressing need for their airplanes to live up to the name <u>bus</u>. It surely can't be that people want to embark/debark a plane with several hundred more people than now and have even more lost bags.

Talk about catering to the bottom line rather than to the comfort and convenience of the passengers. But this is the direction that our air carriers have been taking for years as they gobbled each other up. They have made air travel anathema to most of us… an experience to avoid whenever possible. When my wife and I used to fly to of San Francisco (which is some twelve hours away by car) we experienced the…
* transit times to and from the airport
* security screening
* waiting for the plane to be given a gate
* waiting for boarding to begin
* waiting for the plane to fill

* waiting for takeoff clearance
* the length of the flight, of course
* waiting at baggage pick up
* taking ground transportation to a hotel
* other holdups

With all of these delays, air travel to SF can take about the same amount of time as it does by car. So, why fly and then have to suffer the additional expense and delay of renting a car? Even with the price of gas, the cost of driving is still less than air fare for two. And it immensely more enjoyable if one has the endurance for long distance car travel with occasional stops.

No Class First Class

It has been some time since first class travel on the US airlines has resembled its previous level of comfort and attention. While the seats are about the same, catering to the passengers has fallen off sharply.

On an early evening flight last year our US Airways' first-class meal consisted of multiple bagged snacks and free drinks. This was, however, more than the single bag that was offered to the economy seat patrons. Wow. The stated justification for this lack of service, according to the attendant, was that it was past *their* dinner hour. Sorry, but it was *our* dinner hour. And of course, the airline did not take into consideration that people may be traveling without food to the airport, and then waiting to board during *their* dinner hour.

In 2012 the airlines had decided to reduce the number of first-class seats because 75 percent of them are occupied by mileage-point passengers or by those who upgrade to first class using points. That is a non-revenue scenario that hurts the bottom line, and which leaves the carriers with a limited incentive to provide this comfort. It also, leaves people with additional, unspent mileage points.

Forget that the airlines doled out or had sold points for flying in their planes or using their credit cards. Their contracts to provide seats to is mostly hot air unless you are willing to fly at off-peak times, on circuitous routes, or manage to book one or two of the few seats that they allocate to points passengers on a seemingly random basis. Of course, you can usually get a seat if you cough up two or more times the normal number of points. And this outrage must be well known to the government which does nothing to rein in what I consider a fraud on the public.

And while I'm on the flying topic, what is with the 250-300 pounders who think they can sit in coach seats and overflow fat into their neighbor's space. Just as annoying, besides crying babies, are those who fly in social clusters and think that the fuselage is their private partying room, regardless of the hour. Flying has truly become an unpleasant cattle car experience.

Personal Competition

If you are a Creationist you may not have relevant arguments about the nature and derivation of the behaviors that are exhibited by modern people because we were all created at the same time as our bacteria. But if you examine evolution, it can be useful to give meaning to our social and anti-social traits. The behaviors that we have developed conspire to make us what we are today, like it or not.

One of these negative traits involves competitive behavior. This is an attribute which would normally be deemed to be a positive trait but can occasionally be something else. Whether it is when we are participating in sports, business, or mate selection, some degree of competition is a given, and it is usually constructive.

But competition did not materialize out of thin air or by the grace of God. It became hard-wired into our brains during the search for and the retention of mates, food and security. Those who were most adept at finding and protecting their resources influenced the rest of us by having those beneficial behaviors passed on to successive generations via their genes. If there was no success, there were no successive generations. It could not be more straightforward.

So, competition is a genetic imperative that has been handed down to us even though we have moved further away from the difficulties that led to its development. Today we continue to view these behaviors as being as asset and will sometimes overlook their adverse side effects because of our conditioning. For example, what could be more unacceptable than…
* dog or cock fights
* drinking contests
* bar altercations
* road rage
* professional boxing
* phony wrestling
* assault hockey
* basketball as a contact sport
* the escalating number of fights in the sports arenas

So, it appears that not all competition is productive. The negative side of this activity can also, be observed in the widespread and lightly reported use of illegal drugs in virtually all sports. Since for some winning is not everything, it is the only thing, cheating is a big part of that only thing.

Business Competition

Competition rightfully exists in business, but the fight for consumer dollars can lead to amoral, unethical behaviors in that undertaking such as...
* making secret, anticompetitive deals with other companies
* the solicitation of insider information
* business espionage
* concealing cost saving from alterations to a product's formula

This last item is common way to make a buck by deceiving the public when it is accomplished by reformulating a recipe So, that it...
* may appear to have been improved
* can legally be claimed to be 'new and improved'
* uses fewer and less expensive ingredients without a corresponding reduction in price

Every now and then a company announces that a product contains a 10% (or whatever) increase in some valued ingredient. More than when exactly? Did they also, reduce that particular ingredient over the last months or years only to then be able to tout a contrived improvement? The answer to this question is occasionally yes. How many times over the years have we heard that the same candy bar now has 10% more chocolate? If this were true, without incremental reductions, the bar's weight might a pound by now.

The food industry commonly reduces the amount of an ingredient in a product when wholesale costs escalate… all without informing the public of any change to the product, unless they use the phony new and improved claim (a quality that may rest in the pen of the creative since the feds make no effort to verify it). This lack of meaningful disclosure of a change in ingredients is simple deceit and has been businesses way of doing business for years.

Since corporate non-disclosure occurs with some regularity, one can assume that my negative interpretation of business practices has validity. It would be helpful to see a regulation put in place that would require companies to reveal when an adjustment to a formula has taken place that significantly alters a product. If their recipes are proprietary for valid reasons, they should not have to disclose the exact alterations, but a mandatory notification of some sort might alert the public to any unconstructive change.

Years ago, a chocolate drink powder was introduced using a puffed-up formulation which permitted quicker mixing with milk. Since the objective of the new chemistry was not done to con the public, the puffed-up mix came in a rather large jar at a smaller jar's price. Once its success in the marketplace was recognized, the chemistry was adopted in a preexisting drink mix. Within a short time, the original product was dropped from the store shelves and the newly puffed product was packaged in its original, smaller jar for about the same price as its previous non-puffed powder. So, instead of using two tablespoons to make a glass of chocolate milk, it took three or more… a significant increase to the consumer and profit to the manufacturer.

Eventually the manufacturer returned to what appears to be the original formula packaged in what looks to be the original jar's container size. Apparently there is *not* a sucker born every minute as they expected. Consumer price resistance was probably a factor in this turnabout. Score one for the good guys.

In a similar fashion to the chocolate powder caper above, we should be aware of the puffing of ice cream to the point where in most cases it is essentially frozen air… no exaggeration, more air (sometimes 60% more) than liquid. This weight reduction practice started more than fifty years ago and has continued unabated ever since, with just a few notable exceptions in the super-premium (real ice cream) sector.

With regular ice cream, chemicals such as edible glue have replaced cream as the primary thickener rather than butterfat. And law makers have permitted this reduction in quality to exist without intervention.

FYI - Did you know that low fat ice cream usually contains more sweetener and calories than regular ice cream in order to offset the less desirable taste of what should not be labeled ice cream?

We can thank the efforts of the dairy industry for getting legislators to support their deliberate program of putting less and less of a product in the same size container. Because ice cream is sold by volume, not weight, replacing the solid portion of the ice cream with air does not require a reduction in the container size. Over the years, efforts by consumer advocates have failed to get ice cream sold by its weight (as it rightly should be) due to industry lobbying (bribery).

Can you imagine a can of peaches sold with more juice than fruit and the manufacturer getting away with it? Well, if that wasn't enough of an industry assault on a staple, the half-gallon (2 qt) cartons have been volume-adjusted downward to the current 1.5-quart standard in stages to help obfuscate the change. Apparently the manufactures shamefully figure that the public does not pay attention to product sizing, and they are not far wrong.

If one looks around with a critical eye it is possible to see similar actions being taken industry wide across a broad spectrum of products, and to what good end? When virtually all companies conform to a new, smaller size, or they similarly convert their product to less costly ingredients, they are all in the same boat, competitively speaking. What the chemical industry (who may be the biggest benefactor) supplies to one manufacturer, they can supply to all.

Logic might indicate that this sizing and ingredient modification behavior is actually a stimulating, competitive game, and that businesses enjoy it just for the fun it provides. It certainly can't be that they get off on retooling their production lines from time to time, for no long-term advantage. What ever happened to the effort to get all products delivered in standard sizes or weights anyway?

On the other hand, what resizing, reformulating, and other dodges do is to pump up the potential profit margin So, that the corporations can indulge in the all-to-common practice of running the discounts that are So, attractive to consumers. In industry-speak it is called high/low pricing. To put it another way, companies end up with bloated margins in order to have impressive sales price reductions on some sort of predetermined schedule. But with competition being widespread among manufacturers, everyone is basically on a level playing field, and no one gains any lasting advantage.

The big winners may be the newspapers who get to broadcast the weekly sales with their multi-page ads. The losers are those who receive inferior products or end up paying higher prices in order to support the advertising cost of those recurring discounts.

FYI - When a chef from the Food Channel was asked which olive oil she purchased, her response was "The one that's on sale - one is always on sale". You might do the same for the products you buy.

I suppose there may be a slight advantage to having bloated list prices among those shoppers who are more impressed with their savings than they are with their expenditures. Wouldn't you think that they might get a clue when there are frequent clothing sales of 70% off or more? Do they think that these businesses are in the money losing trade?

Peripheral issues to contrived sales are the grocery and cosmetic coupons that are touted by newspaper and Internet sites. Essentially these are offers to induce customers to buy things that they may not need or want. I am amused when a housewife is shown saving $100 or more with her shopping cart full of items. Virtually all of those grocery coupons are for junk food and not for healthy, fresh, or fresh frozen foods.

Going back to sizing. When I was a kid the large potato chip box was 16 ounces in weight from virtually every vendor. Gradually, so that few might take notice, the size of the inner bag in the box was reduced ounce by ounce. Eventually when the smaller bags looked silly in the box and became too small in size to be convenient for the homemaker, a colossal, new 1 pound box was introduced. This downsizing and upsizing has happened many times over the years because so few pay attention to, or object to the manipulation of the consumer.

At one time the 14.5 ounce can of vegetables was 16 ounces. And why is it 14.5 ounces anyway? Well, do the math. Actually, doing the math is the problem because this odd sizing game makes price comparisons more difficult. The conversions to obtuse sizing have become So, flagrant that grocery stores may include a cost-per-ounce or similar listings on their shelf labels for those with the inclination to use them. Do we need more proof than this that manufactures are working to obfuscate their pricing to the public?

Then there is the cosmetic industry. This is a large group of companies that have taken prevarication to new lows. Recently it was the essence of avocado that did wonders. Before that is was milk and botanicals. Then it was mushrooms. Oh no, not any ordinary mushrooms, but Portobello mushrooms… presumably because they are known to be a gourmet treat. We can only hope that it will not be garlic's or cabbages' turn next.

Business Rip Offs

In 2010 it was reported that several insurance companies had taken advantage of the relatives of deceased soldiers. They managed the death benefits, earned some 5% on these accounts, and then paid out about 1% in interest to the relatives. The retained difference amounted to healthy windfall for this handful of companies. A class action suit was eventually initiated to recover these ill-gotten gains. This again shows how big business can be corrupted by its quest for ever greater profits.

In 2012 a superstorm named Sandy smashed into the East Coast of the US. Flood insurance companies, working with FEMA, sent an army of engineers to investigate its damage. Their assigned task was to discover how much of the devastation to policy holder's homes was caused by the surging seawater and how much of it predated the storm.

More than two years later a group of lawyers that are representing about 1500 homeowners are attempting to prove that a number of the engineering firms that were hired to inspect the damage issued false reports in order to give insurers sufficient justification to deny claims. For example, some broken home foundations were allegedly blamed on poor construction or on settling of the soil. In other cases, cracked or warped walls were being attributed to the building's old age. As of 2015 the verdict is not yet in.

The home/small-office printer and ink cartridge business is an excellent case of an all-too-clever business plan with their: set prices low now, get large profits in the future scheme… one that we should all be aware of. There are also, many other companies that function in this devious way. The game is to price the non-disposable part of a product near or below the cost of manufacture to encourage sales, then make up for the tiny profit or initial loss with the highly profitable, disposable items that are used by these products. Printers and ink cartridges are a part of this notorious business plan. In a few cases these printers have actually priced below the cost of replacement printer cartridges. In one particular case that I noted, a new printer was priced at about 30 percent less that its cartridges.

For my printing needs I have chosen to purchase cartridges from a third-party supplier at a discount. The potential downside to this method of replacement can be the loss of warranty (who cares) and the products may shorten a printer's lifespan (not likely). I have experienced a few faulty cartridges that were replaced for free but have not yet had a printer issue.

In 2013 Anheuser-Busch was accused, in a $5 million, false-labeling, class-action lawsuit, of watering down its beer. Their labels state 5% as the alcohol content for the regular beer, while some light versions are said to be 4+%. However, it is alleged that the alcohol content has been reduced by 3 to 8 percent with the addition of water to the batches after normal brewing. Since the manufacturing tax fees vary based on the amount of alcohol in a product, I wonder if A-B notified the government of the change to reduce their taxes. It is likely they were just content having to brew less alcohol for their dollar intake.

Absence of Standards

As a beginning programmer I was expected to learn the coding standards for software So, that the end-user would not be required to guess or research what to do next when running my program. For the most part, our community has generally improved somewhat on these techniques over the years. As a result, software usually functions in a similar, reasonable way from program to program. When using a program, if I am required to read the instructions before running the software, I know that the programmer or analyst had not done their job well.

Other industries are another matter. Perhaps the most glaring absence of standards is with the electronics industry's remote-control units, whether for the DVD player, surround sound, or the TV itself. Those who are employed to design these devices apparently lock themselves in window-less, phone-less, rooms without meaningful contact with the outside world, except during bathroom breaks. The result is what one might expect. There is little rhyme or reason to the button layouts from one manufacturer to the next. And remotes do not function with other manufacturer's products. And why not? There is no reasonable answer to that query.

What must surely be the worst case of remotes-out-of-control are the TV/DVD controllers which can be found in hotels and resorts. Even with my background in electronics, using these devices is anything but simple. I imagine that the hotel's engineers are driven crazy having to repeatedly explain the functions and missing functions to the guests.

To a lesser degree, the automobile industry functions in a similar mode. Driving a different car should not mean having to retrieve the operating manual or suffer minutes of concentration before one embarks. Yet being an occasional rental customer, I know this expectation is a flight of fancy. Try to figure out how to manipulate the windshield wiper control for a very light rain sometime.

It's not as if having product designers who are trained to observe the consensus of standards were an insurmountable process. It just requires a little communication and compromise with others in the same industry. But companies behave like the political parties do… the other guys are their mortal enemies. It's a worse than silly position, and like politics, their attitudes makes it our loss.

Another absence of standards revolves around the way in which items are rated. Years back a problem surfaced when companies were stating their size of computer video displays. Eventually a universal, diagonal measurement was settled on after disgruntled consumers played the lawyer card.

Today, flat screen television sets and monitors are another example of a standard's issue. One of the common measurements of quality resides in the contrast ratio (the difference between pure black and pure white), but not all manufactures use the same testing algorithm (mathematical formula) to calculate this measurement. One company's stated ratio of 25.000 to 1 may be better than another company's ratio of 50.000 to 1. And it is not as if the one with the deceptive rating does not know what they are doing. But because the government does not oversee this process, the manufacturers feel free to fudge the numbers without fear of retribution… again, until someone plays the lawyer card.

Excessive Promotion

If I were to identify the one business that is the most corrupt from a consumer aspect it would be the cosmetics industry. Virtually nothing that they tout to be miracle skin rejuvenation products is even modestly effective, but this does nothing to stop new remedies from regularly being added to their advertising budgets. When the initial flood of purchases dies off and they become uneconomical to promote, it's on to the next name in this name-game scenario.

Every now and then one of these companies (usually of modest size) develops an aggressive business plan that is intended to take it into the big leagues. A few years back a cosmetics company created its variety of products for consumers. Then they went on a spending binge with an immense advertising budget and unsubstantiated claims to capture a share of this large segment. A research article indicated that this company was spending 85% of its income on advertising and only 15% on their products, company administration, and debt. Based on how little they allocated to R&D it's likely that their products consisted of easily purchased ingredients and did not represent cutting edge anything. The advertising blitz went on for a few years, and then just as quickly as they came on the scene they dropped off of the map, probably when too many consumers discovered that their wares did not live up to the hype.

In 2014 members of the automobile insurance industry had begun engaging in this same breakout tactic… massive, dishonest ads to obtain a bigger slice of a large pie. Since huge budgets are being directed into these campaigns, how much can be left over for filling auto claims fairly, or for the unbelievable rate savings that are claimed. And how can they *all* be cheaper than the others?

Deceitful Promotion

The propaganda surrounding product advertising has for some time been used to promote their industries as being beneficial to the consumer. It alleges to introduce us to new products and exposes us to what we might need to know. Without advertising, So, the story goes, many good ideas might languish in the minds of their creators and not become known to the public.

Unfortunately, the bad comes hand in hand with the alleged good. This is because there is only minimal government intervention into the deceptive practices of business. Corporations are free to extol the nonexistent virtues that they assign to their products without fear of contradiction or retribution. In some cases, this deception takes the form of its packaging graphics. That is, the paper and ink package presentation of a product may have little connection to the contents that are inside.

Some foods use manicured "serving suggestion" pictures on the outside of the box, or they may offer the equally deceptive "enlarged to show detail" statement in their ads. How these images relate to what is on the inside a package or what the actual sizing of an item is must reside in a purchaser's imagination.

In a similar vein some years ago, a major soup manufacturer was discovered putting clear marbles in bottom of its televised soup bowls So, that the solid ingredients would sit near the surface and look more substantial. And what was the punishment for this unrealistic display? It was a cease-and-desist order. That's all. Not exactly a stinging rebuke that might deter the next company from perpetrating such a fraud.

Also, years ago the milk industry came up with a slogan for an ad campaign that promoted milk as "Nature's most nearly perfect food". This advertising ran for months before the misstatement of fact was forced off of the airwaves. Later they were back with the catchy phrase of "Good for every body", and again they were required to retract their ads. More recently, milk had been promoted as having a beneficial effect on dieting. And again, they were required to delete these commercials because of having no evidence to support their dubious contention. They just don't give up, do they?

These ongoing efforts by industries don't surprise me because there is virtually no economic downside to these calculated misstatements of fact. Their message can be removed from circulation, but the public may remember it and never realize that it was nothing more than a clever marketing phrase with no scientific support, and that the misstatement of fact had been forced off of the airwaves.

So, the FDA issues their directive, and that is the end of it. No public rebuke, rarely an order for corrective advertising, generally no fines or other penalties, just a brief interruption in corrupt business-as-usual.

One extremely rare exception to the slap on the wrist was a juice packager that made misleading claims about their products. They were subsequently required to purchase a substantial amount corrective advertising. So, what did they do? Did they have to explain that they had lied? No. They were permitted to advertise that their juice had a certain, small percent of real fruit juice as if that was an advantage to the consumer. After a run of these corrective ads and a loss of consumer interest, this particular item dropped off the map. Maybe the public can see, just don't hold your breath.

Excessive and fraudulent commercials are more evidence of how the government is run by big business.

A government/business promotion that dwarfed much of industries advertising was the elevation of corn to rock star status in the search for sustainable energy sources. Yes…
* like other grains it can produce ethanol
* we still have some suitable land left that can be used for additional corn production
* we do need alternative sources of fuel if we are not going to reduce our dependence on foreign energy
* it would benefit some farmers (especially the already prosperous agribusiness farms with millions of planted acres)

But what almost no one tells us is that…

* ethanol has a 30% less energy content than gasoline (to be fair, ethanol is 113 octanes, and if cars were specifically tuned for this with a higher compression ratio and more substantial plumbing, the energy output would become equivalent, but that has not happened)
* the energy in a gallon of ethanol is only marginally more than the energy that is needed to produce it (a study by Cornell University stated that it takes 1.3 gallons of oil to produce 1 gallon of ethanol when every aspect of production and delivery is considered)
* the price of corn, corn products, and corn fed for livestock has escalated as corn's new demand moved it from corn-the-food-crop toward corn-the-energy-crop
* the agribusiness corn producers are the big winners
* politicians benefit from the massive amounts of money that are diverted from the loose pockets of agribusiness
* demand for oil and all of the ills that accompany it goes on virtually unabated

If the above is not convincing enough, consider that a full-sized SUV requires 450 pounds of corn in order to yield enough ethanol to fill its tank. That is 450 pounds of a crop that cannot be of benefit to us elsewhere, including foreign exchange. And this use of corn has driven up the prices of feed animals and the consumer products that rely on corn. Some proof of this is that in the fall of 2011 the price of corn had risen 16 percent over the previous year. Have you noticed beef prices lately?

Deceitful Representation

From fast food to frozen food, figures don't lie, but liars sure can figure. According to news reports these industries are Well, known for underrating the calorie counts of their products by as much as 30%. The government may require posting this information on a label or a wall, but apparently they have no inclination to verify the results. Perhaps they figure a close call is sufficient for consumers to make informed judgments. Or more likely it is that they assume their going through the motions of industry oversight will keep us off of their backs. Also, does lobbying come to mind?

What could be more dishonest than the blizzard of phony claims and intentionally misleading statements that are made on a daily basis by the food, cosmetic, and other industries? Quasi-terms and labels are invented to sound meaningful but may have no basis in English or in any facts that they might imply.

Perhaps the most abused word is natural. There is no legal definition to this word, but it is freely used to impart the illusion of goodness to many products. Have you ever bought a natural hair spray? What exactly could be natural about hair spray? Is there a hair spray plant somewhere that I don't know about?

Virtually every ad on television is laced with some degree of sounds-impressive-but-says-nothing verbiage to deceive and manipulate consumers. A buyer's judgment should be that if it sounds too good it is probably a prevarication.

Mark Twain: *"Get your facts first, and then you can distort em as much as you please."*

As one example among many, a cosmetics company uses a coined word in their advertising that is similar to regenerate. According to the dictionary *their* word means... oops, the word is not in the dictionary. It was created for the illusionary effect that it could produce in the mind of the consumer. A product with regenerative qualities must surely accomplish something, right?

A number of companies use this faux-word technique because of the gullibility of consumers and the recognition of this by the advertisers. In recent years there have been a number of new ice-cream-like names that are used for what we might assume to be real ice cream but are not. If you churn something, isn't it ice cream? These invented, cutie, names are used So, that the label does not have to disclose something like This product does not even come close to being real ice cream.

An often-abused word is fresh. It may or may not mean what you think it does, and this term reaches the zenith of obfuscation with the term fresh frozen. So, is it fresh or is it frozen? Is it frozen while fresh as opposed to being frozen after rotting? Many of us will recognize the dichotomy of juxtaposing these two words, but this does nothing to prevent food companies from utilizing advertising doublespeak to influence those who are easily misled.

Another highly deceptive use of words is to describe a product using the term made *with*. This widespread and misleading phraseology works to a manufacturer's advantage because the average person will assume they are being told that a product is basically made <u>of</u> some ingredient or material, when in fact they are being told no such thing. *Made_of* means composed of a single ingredient. *Made_with* carries no such denotation. It only means that it contains <u>some</u> of an ingredient.

One restaurant chain claimed that their burgers were made with three, desirable, cuts of prime beef. And of course, they do not say how much of each is used. Is it 3% or 33%? We don't actually know because the intention of the ad was meant to mislead, not inform. These folks rightfully figure that people may assume that there is some sort of even ingredients split in the burgers. The ad further suggests that their burgers taste better than those that are made from other (and perhaps just as tasty) cuts. That is another non-justified statement that is also, meant to impress but not inform.

Then there is the breakfast syrup that is no longer made with any butter as its name implies. When it first came out it specified having 2% butter on its ingredients list. Now that the consumers may have become aware of its butter content and taste, that component has been reduced to 0%. So, did the manufacturer disclose this significant change, other than its absence from the ingredients list? Did they remove the word butter from the name? Nope. Instead, it now claims that the product is buttery, in its ads. So, apparently a claim of being buttery and not actually containing any butter is ok with the manufacturer and the feds, even if it may not be ok with the rest of us.

One of the pet food purveyors claims that their dog food "Does not contain any *added* hormones". Would this surprise anyone? Do companies buy hormones by the bucket So, that they can add it to their prepared food? Aren't hormones given to feed animals to increase their growth potential? Please note that the company in question did not claim that their food did *not* contain any hormones. They also, stated that their pet food does not contain any *added* antibiotics. Same story here.

Many of the products that we buy have a similar, cavalier, attitude toward the dispensing the truth. Misleading the public, it seems, is not against the law, as witnessed by the fact that there are So, many corporations indulging in this practice. And it gives the 'creatives' something to do for a living.

Another product has also, succumbed to the shrink the size rather than raise the price strategy. I picked up a quart of mayonnaise at the grocery and discovered that their standard jars are now only 15 and 30 ounces in size. Can 13 and 26 ounces be far away?

On the soft drink front, a small soda carrier holds 6 bottles or cans of the beverage. The next size upholds double that, or 12 bottles or cans as we might expect. With this established progression in mind, one would not be blamed for assuming that the next larger packaging size would contain 24. Nope! It holds only 20… 4 short of doubling the previous size. At first glance the large case might even look like it holds 24 containers with its long, thin, (purposely deceiving?) design. This is probably what the vendors would like you to think when you try to compute its cost per bottle or can. Let's see… if

12 sodas cost $4.95 and 20 cost $8.49, quick - which is the better value?

An area that seems to be on the increase is store brand pricing. While most of us would expect this to be an area where bargains can be found, it may not always be the case. Apparently the chain stores are finding this to be a nice profit center for them. In addition, there may be some deception involved in the packaging. I noticed that one stores pasta boxes were the same size as a popular brand, but the contents were 12 ounces, not the normal 16 ounces, making the cost per ounce higher for the store's product during the frequent sales of the name brand box.

An article in a scientific magazine alleged that the holistic or health formula industry had virtually no products that were or could be proven to be either safe or effective. But you wouldn't know this from looking at the health-store shelves that are packed with 'cures and remedies. And do the consumers of these products really know anything about them that does not come from highly unreliable word of mouth of clerks and some users?

Because these formulas are not drugs (they are legally foods), the government does little to regulate their implied (or explicit by the word of salesclerks) benefits to the consumer. I wonder. Could the Justice Department, the FTC, or the

FDA ever consider their false advertising as sufficient justification for prosecution? Apparently it is easier for these agencies to ignore the billions spent by the easily duped public then to stop this rampant consumer fraud through law enforcement. I don't suppose that lobbying has played any role in this charade, as well.

Why is it that we are disposed to forcefully restrict those harmless activities that offend some people's moral compass, but are unwilling to deter the every-day, white-collar criminals? Surely we cannot believe that false advertising is victimless, or that those who are duped deserve what they get.

In one particularly egregious case of not-really-saying-anything advertising, a company's package wording *implies* that it prevents colds from airborne contagions. The problem is that implying is not the same as a direct statement, and it cannot easily be litigated against as a false writing. Their original packaging entreated us to "Take at the first sign of a cold symptom or before entering crowded environments". This is not exactly a promise for it to accomplish anything, is it? Then in print So, small that you may not be able to, or are not interested in reading it, they say "This product is not intended to diagnose, treat, cure or prevent the common cold". So, then what is it? Well, it's one hell of a money maker, that's what. Then in an attempt to turn their product's liability into an asset, the packaging shouts that it was "Created by a second-grade schoolteacher" as if this tidbit of information should be convincing to anyone with more than a second-grade education. Perhaps this female creator had assistance in developing the product from her scriptwriter (no kidding) husband.

To date, there is no cure for the common cold and apparently no cure for the common sucker, either.

Again, in the not-really-saying-anything department, commercials may start out with a statement talking about how consumers want to save money. One would not be faulted for expecting that the subsequent dialog would have something to do with savings in the following few seconds. But a lack of follow-up information on that particular subject happens far too often, and we are left with a savings-implication that is less than worthless.

If consumers paid critical attention to the multitude of advertising lies, I suspect there would be less of them.

Deceitful Incentives

A product commercial on TV may include the stipulation that it is available for only a limited time. Infomercials invariably express the condition that their offer has a short duration (just like timeshare salespersons do). Oh sure. That's why these same commercials run over and over containing the same time restrictions. They apparently learned this false enticement style from auto salesmen.

This may not apply to every airline mileage card, but it did to ours and probably does to yours. The bankcard's advertising claimed to provide a coach class ticket to anywhere they fly in the US with an accumulation of 25.000 points. No blackouts, no holiday restrictions, virtually all cities. So, far, So, good, right? Well, there is a downside that must be tucked away in the fine print of their contract (you know, the details that nobody reads).
* if the ticket is for a short hop that an airline carrier may normally charge 15.000 points for, you still pay with 25.000 points
* tickets are dispensed from the airline's class of least desirable seats with departure times like 6:00am and 6:00pm
* if an early or late departure is an unacceptable burden, the flyer can pay extra fee (we experienced $90 up-charge in one case and $150 in another) per person to receive a more favorable departure time
* apparently the bank that we *had* our card with would purchase the cheapest tickets in the marketplace, So, our flight from Phoenix to New

Orleans went through Atlanta with a long delay… say, isn't Atlanta on the other side of New Orleans from Phoenix?

Then there are the catches incumbent with airline-specific mileage card programs. I attempted to book a flight to Hawaii using points six months in advance of the trip. Initially I was told that those seats were not yet available, the agent didn't know when they would be, and told me to continue checking back. What, every day for six months? On contacting customer service, I was told that the 35.000-point seats had been available for 240 days before the flight date and that they had been sold out. However, I could fly for 70.000 points per seat if I wanted… on the same flight and date. The moral of this story is to plan your holiday Well, in advance to obtain the few seats that are allocated to mileage-points redemption.

Follow-up: In attempting to book two mileage-points flights to New Orleans the following year, I started checking for availability 240 days out as I had previously been instructed. As you might guess, there were no seats available on any flight on or around my preferred departure and return dates, much less at a convenient time of day. After a few days of surfing their web site, a phone call to customer service informed me that those seats are freed up based on a proprietary algorithm (mathematical formula) that looks at how fast the plane is filling up. Big demand for seats equals few or no mileage seats. However, I could book a 25.000-point flight for 60.000 points each... or more than double the fictional seats. On further checking I discovered first class accommodations to our location were available for 50.000 points each. A no-brainer for me.

Deceitful Banking

If you have been paying attention you may have noticed that there is a proliferation of TV ads for checking-account-connected debit cards. I'm not quite sure why anyone would want one of these cards unless its sole purpose is to limit a child's away-from-home spending to the amount allotted to their account by the parents. Short of that kind of control, I must be missing the point. Don't credit cards work in basically the same way without these particular limits? Maybe people get debit cards because they have no credit.

A bank's financial justification for the costly promotion of these cards can have only one purpose, and that is to increase its revenues. Ordinarily that might not be a negative scenario, but a portion of the additional revenue is achieved by expecting their cardholders to mistakenly overdraw their bank accounts and incur penalty fees.

Something like one third all purchases are now made with a debit card. Knowing the average consumer's proclivity for misjudging their account balance, bank income must be substantial. In addition, some banks do not permit consumers to opt out of the included overdraft protection plan to eliminate insufficient-balance coverage and penalties. As a result, the cards can be used until denied, regardless of their negative balance. Nice! And of course, some of these same practices apply to checking accounts. Overdraft fees can range from $10 to $35 or more if the balance is not brought up to date quickly or is highly overdrawn.

One particularly egregious revenue-generating aspect of the bank's overdraft procedures can be to pay the incoming checks beginning with the largest ones first when there are several presented for processing on the same day. What this does is insure that the client incurs the maximum number of bounced checks. In this scenario a single large check could cause several smaller checks to bounce whereas only one check needed to bounce if the largest were considered last. When questioned about this policy, the bank's rationale was that large checks are probably more important to the customer and should be paid first. You bet.

Note: This practice is now illegal.

Banks should be in business of protecting their client's assets, not to plundering them with high fees and other harmful practices.

Another way the banks bilk the consumer is with changes in the interest rates that they charge. You may qualify for a nominal rate, say around 8-10%, and then have it changed to a much higher rate because you applied elsewhere for an additional credit card or two... perhaps for the sole purpose of receiving a 10% discount on first-day purchases at a department store. So, taking advantage of those deals can be very costly indeed. Sometimes it results in the doubling or tripling your previous interest rate for no legitimate reason. The rational (sure) may be that receiving additional cards extends your potential debt and is a warning flag (or is it a target?) for the banks.

Be aware that *potential* debt can be assessed as negatively as is *actual* debt by both the credit reporting agencies and by the banks.

To compound matters, banks appear to be ratcheting down a billing cycle's grace period to twenty-one days... down from what had been the industry standard of twenty-five days. And the banks may be in no big rush to get your statement in the mail. We have seen ours take up to ten days in transit from its closing date. So, it's not enough that the credit card companies make a healthy fee on transactions, but they want more, and will think up new ways to get it.

In addition to questionable banking practices, there are the unfair policies of...
* double cycle billing in which lenders calculate one month's interest fees based on two months of activity the <u>first</u> time that a less than full payment is made
* allocating customer payments to the charges that have the lowest interest rate (assuming that the account had been charged different rates at different times, even if the higher rate came first) and therefore earning more from the higher interest rate

Let us say that you pay off your credit card debt on time each month. Then you inadvertently pay one dollar less than the full amount that is due or are one day late due to mistake or slow mail delivery. The following month you go right back to paying in full. Any reasonably intelligent person would assume that there would be an interest charge for just one month. Wrong. The banks will charge interest two months in a row - potentially doubling your interest rate for that period, and it's all legal. This is patently unfair, but there is no one on your side to stop it.

If you have a $5000 balance at 9% interest rate and then accept a teaser rate of 0% on a $7000 balance transfer (which converts to 18% in six months). Payments will be applied to the $5000 portion of the indebtedness that is being charged the 9% interest. This may sound reasonable at first, but the effect is that the interest on the $7000 is coming ever closer and is at 18%. This becomes an interest landfall for the banks, otherwise why would they offer the teaser?

Note: In 2010 a law took effect that addressed bank policies. While this went some distance toward fairness, it was hardly circumspect. Even before the regulations became law, the banks were busy inventing new ways to enhance their revenue, such as by increasing interest rates on those who do *not* have a payment problem. In addition, those who pay their balances off every month may be subjected to an activity fee, or those who do not use their card regularly, to an inactivity fee. I imagine that this is going to be a hit against American Express as cardholders shed those cards that are not universally accepted. There may also, be reluctance to waive any first-time overdraft fees or late charges. In 2009 the banks made $39 billion on this service, and it's likely to increase.

One item that missed the 2010 law is how credit card credits are handled. American Express reduces the balance owed on transactions as soon as the credit has been processed. Visa, on the other hand, does not consider your incoming credits until the next billing cycle. What this means is that you have to initially pay for those items that were returned in one cycle, and then wait to have your statement credited on the next cycle. This is a major windfall for Visa when you consider this huge amount of month-to-month float as an interest free loan to them.

Because of low inflation and banking overhead, interest rates on CDs are pathetically low, or about a penny on the dollar annually. Unless you have a lot of cash lying around, keeping it in a sock under your mattress is not a bad idea.

The kicker that seems to go with obtaining money from a bank or delivering money to a bank is the omnipresent disclaimer: This offer may be withdrawn at the discretion of the bank at any time. So, why is it that a contract allows the bank off the hook at their whim and not the customer? I suggest two possible options for the consumer with these documents. Have the bank remove the offending wording or go somewhere else.

In 2011 the Federal Reserve was assigned the task of setting the rates (card swipe fees) that bankcard processors could charge for their debit and credit transactions. The idea was to have them more closely reflect the cost of processing. Fees typically ran 2-3 percent for credit cards and 1-2 percent for debit cards, and the cost to the consumer (indirectly) had grown to $40 billion dollars in 2009.

For years merchants have been complaining that the rates were too high and forced prices up to cover them. When the Fed proposed limiting bank fees to 12 cents per transaction, the lobbyists got into high gear. One of their claims was that the retailers wanted the consumer rather than themselves to foot the bill. To which I would have to observe that this is what they already do with higher product pricing.

In what may have been posturing, the financial institutions said they might have to stop issuing these cards. Because of the lost income, several banks said they will begin charging debit card holders a monthly fee. So, it appears that consumers may not win the fight for fair fees no matter what the feds decided.

In 2012 a consolidate set of suits against the credit card companies shot down the provision that vendors who accept their cards could not charge customers less for paying cash. Now they may do as they please, and we will see how that plays out for consumers. It will be a difficult decision for the vendors because so many people use credit cards, and they may not have an appetite for increased costs.

It turns out that Bankcard companies don't just do the banks bidding. They also, play unfairly among themselves. MasterCard and Visa were required in 2008, via settlement of a lawsuit, to pay American Express nearly $4 billion dollars because of their antitrust violations. AmEx had accused a credit card processor of conspiring with MasterCard and Visa to discourage their client banks from issuing Amex cards. This shows how fierce competition for the dollar warps the perspective of big business and encourages the sleaze to come out of the woodwork.

We should note that no individual from Visa, MasterCard, or the processing company was fined or sent to prison. Perhaps AmEx concurred with the court that this is *just business*, like lines from the Sopranos and other Mafia works.

Bankcard companies also, play fast and loose with the credit card's business customers. When they are paid with a credit card, the transaction debits their buyer's account immediately. But what about paying the seller? They may not get their money until three days later, which amounts to an interest windfall for the bankcard folks. If you tally up how many transactions occur per day and multiply that by an average transaction amount, then total that for the three days that they can invest the vendor's money, interest revenue is significant. And of course, it is not shared with the seller who has to wait for his money.

Another way that banks work against people with debt is when they are permitted to manipulate interest rates at their discretion. In the distant past there were usury laws that limited the amount of interest a lender could charge to a borrower to 24%. Now apparently all bets are off because rates in the high 20s and occasionally in the 30's are not uncommon because revolving credit is not considered a loan. Really? Good job lobbyists. And with debt at an all-time high, this has become a big bonus for the lenders. Wouldn't you like to borrow money for a few percent and then lend it out for 25 or 30%? Who needs loan sharks when we have bank sharks?

Banks also, use the: subject to change disclaimer to alter your credit card contract at will. And of course, this is done without your advice and consent because they know that you might not agree.

Going hand in hand with rate obscenity are these contract rules that few of us ever read, until it is too late. For example, if you are late with a car payment, an unrelated credit card company may have the right to double or triple your interest rate on your account with *them*.

The same might be true if some other credit history that you have is not perfect. Imagine that you have $10.000 of debt on a credit card and inadvertently miss the due date on some *other* payment. When this is transmitted to the credit reporting agencies, your credit card company is also, privy to that information, and they may invoke their fine print rule #999 where they can arbitrarily increase your interest rate, even though there was no credit offense against their institution. If this happens, the interest burden that you may have been able to manage on the $10.000 debt might now become unmanageable. This is all because the credit bureaus can transmit your information freely (ok so, far) and the banks can use it as they see fit (not ok), and all with virtually no oversight from the government.

Bank Corruption

In 2014 Citigroup, J P Morgan, Chase, Royal Bank of Scotland, HSBC Bank, and USB agreed to a settlement with the various regulating agencies in several countries that totaled just under 3.4 billion dollars. For years these institutions had used their internet communications to manipulate <u>and</u> brag about rigging the currency markets. This regulatory action came on the heels of an investigation of a similar scandal where various financial institutions were involved in illegally fixing the London Inter-bank offered rate or LIBOR.

In addition, the US Treasury Department announced that they were fining the largest US banks 950 million dollars for failing to prevent misconduct in their foreign-exchange trading operations. This manipulation of the exchange rates has "a profound effect on the economy" according to the CFTC director. Apparently was not deemed So profound that a more hefty fine was imposed. $1 billion is chump change to these institutions.

So, there are several things that should be apparent here. The banks have demonstrated that they feel that they are above the law, and they were even arrogant enough to brag about their misdeeds on social media sites. Apparently, once again with big business, no one has done jail time for their parts in this banking fraud. While $3.4 billion and $950 million may sound like very large penalties to most of us, they amount to little more than a slap on the wrist for the cash rich banks that were fined. Therefore, the fines offer little incentive against future manipulations by those officers and corporations that were involved.

Censorship Express

I have taken the position that censorship, short of not being able to scream fire in a theater, is not productive, and it is not for anyone to promote or impose. But there are those who just can't stand to mind their own business.

In 2012 PayPal, the major Internet transaction processor for the credit card companies, dictated to Smashwords (part of Amazon), an Internet publisher, that they must remove all of the books from their inventory that deal with incest, bestiality, and rape, or they would be denied PayPal's payment transfer services. This threat carries a lot of weight because of how important their services are to publishers and independent writers. While the credit card processors that are behind the PayPal initiative were not disclosed at this time, it is likely, according to Smashwords, that it was probably all of them.

One has to wonder at why restricting the publishing of legal books would be on the agenda of these companies. How is it that they feel the need to interject themselves into this arena? Aren't there enough pressing problems in this country without big business putting their religious noses into legitimate writings? Censorship is an obscenity that should not be tolerated by any society. And if these businesses were to win this battle, where does their war end. Didn't we learn a lesson from the book burnings in Hitler's Germany?

On the good news front, a few weeks after the fallout from their decision hit the fan, PayPal saw the light (emails, letters, editorials, phone calls) and essentially reversed their decision.

On the bad new front, there was a very public book burning of piles of three books in an author's series that included a good deal of very hot sex. One of the males interviewed over this event complained that the books made it impossible for men to live up to the new expectations, as if these novels became a woman's bibles. My take is… how do meatheads like this ever get their 15 minutes of shame? Oh yea. It's that sex repression thing again.

Back to Banks

The bankers lobbied congress a few years back to dramatically tighten the criteria for exercising bankruptcy that resulted from their own loose credit and debt transfers policies? So, have you homesteaded your home in those states which allow it? If not, do it now! This is a consumer protection feature that prevents institutions from attaching a specified amount (up to 100%) of the value of your home to service your debt, should you exercise personal bankruptcy. You may have $100.000 or more in home equity dollars that are exempt from credit company seizure. Once the bankruptcy proceeding are over, you could sell your home, recover the equity, and the lenders cannot touch it.

Disclaimer... since I am not a lawyer, you are advised to seek appropriate legal counsel in order to verify my understanding of the law. Ok? And don't you just love it that I have to say this for something So, straightforward?

One final indictment against the banking industry. When the financial institutions were consolidating and misrepresenting the risk of their predatory (insufficient homeowner income) loan packages, the banks were complicit by selling them forward (and taking commissions) to Fanny Mae and Freddy Mac (FM/FM). Then some of them took bail-out money from the feds to stay above water when the housing collapse occurred.

In 2011 the Federal Housing Finance Agency (FHFA), with the jurisdiction to oversee FM/FM, sued seventeen major banks which were instrumental in some $200 billion in losses. Their suit alleged that these banks broke state and federal laws with their loan package sales. The FHFA alleged that these home mortgage-backed securities (derivatives) had been marketed with registration statements and prospectuses that "contained materially false or misleading statements and omission'". Regardless of the outcome, my bet is that none of those culpable in this scandal will ever be required to enter into restitution by returning their commissions, or by facing jail time. Wait and see.

Going hand and hand with the housing crisis are the incredible lines in the sand that have been drawn by mortgage banks. Rather than renegotiate their high interest-rate loans, they have mostly chosen to turn out owners who could have managed their debt if the interest rates had been lowered. So, instead of promoting good relationships with the communities and maintaining a steady flow of income, these banks saw fit to evict people and shoot themselves in the foot.

In some cases where the homeowners made an effort to negotiate their monthly payments down, bank policies prevented them from even talking about doing a deal unless the homeowners were delinquent in their payments. Yep! Talk about self-inflicted wounds.

While there are reasons why the housing crisis occurred, this ongoing foolishness has exacerbated the problem rather than resolve it. And those of us who were not part of this difficulty have seen their home values plummet as well.

Whistleblowers would not be needed in government or business if there were not rampant, corrupt practices going on.

Major corporations would like us to imagine that it is the politicians who are doing (usually preventing) the public's bidding, but nothing could be further from the truth. A few of the real power brokers involved in this action are the...

* financial institutions
* communications institutions
* military industrial complex
* automobile industries
* health insurance industries
* pharmaceutical industries
* agricultural industries
* oil, gas & coal industries

Executive Embellishment

I suppose for the elite there can be made a case made for excessive executive compensation. They are in the upper echelons of business and feel that they deserve to be there. In addition, they believe that their contribution to the business far exceeds the small fraction that they receive... i.e. a small piece of a much bigger pie. Maybe you even buy into this self-serving philosophy.

For most of us, our permissiveness with corporate selfishness has led us to circumstances where we sit quietly in the shadows while the business executives make (not earn) thousands of times what the government sets as the minimum wage. Lehman Brothers, in one particular case, paid a consultant nearly $1.000.000 *per day* for 17 days just prior to their receiving $billions in a Fed bailout.

Along the same lines, Goldman Sachs Group, Inc. (GSG) seems to have become a breeding ground for unrestrained corruption with their all's fair in business attitude… a concept that inexorably flows down from the top of the management ladder. And their deficiencies in fair play are not isolated examples. Executives at the top pay scales have historically shown little regard for their worker's compensation in comparison to their own. The disparity between one's actual worth to a company and their good-ol'-boy network of inflated salaries has been getting more egregious over the years.

In 2013 once again, an activist group has tendered a shareholder proposal to have GSG adopt an independent Board Chairman who has not had affiliations with the bank. GSG's traditional response in these matters has been to ask the SEC to exclude the proposal from its proxy. The subject of chairman independence has become a hot topic among corporation investors these days, but their success rates have been mixed. GSG, with its efforts, has managed to beat back a series of these proposals to date.

Merrill Lynch is reputed to have remodeled its executive's office a while back for an incoming

CEO to the tune of $1.2 million. This included chairs for about $15.000 each, a $35.000 toilet, a $1.400 trash can. This is more than the average price of five homes in 2007 dollars. And we haven't touched on his golden parachute, country club membership, chauffeured limousine, executive jet, stock options, and oh yes, base income. Their chauffeur service alone ran some $230.000. Aint life grand at the top?

In 2012 a portion of the Dodd-Frank package on financial reform, which has been labeled an internal equity provision, obligates board members to take into consideration the differential between their executive's pay and the average salary of the company's employees. In recent years, executive pay packages have been rising faster than the inflation index. I guess even the Republicans have had enough of this out-of-control trend. Of course, looking at an issue is certainly no guarantee that these boards will act to change an outrageous ratio.

Insider Trading Deals

In 2010 Rajat Gupta, a director at GSG, was charged with leaking secrets about the bank's dealings to a hedge fund. One of his insider tips was that Berkshire Hathaway was about to shore up GSG during the financial crisis. In 2012 presiding Judge Rakoff said that this was "disgusting in its implications" and "a terrible breach of trust". So, what was the sentence handed down for such a heinous crime? It was two years (probably to be at some clubhouse jail if the sentence is even upheld) and a five million dollar fine (which is chump change to people at this level of banking).

Since 2009 six former SAC Capitol Advisors (founder Steven A Cohen) employees have been convicted of insider trading. Four are now cooperating with the government, and a seventh was indicted in 2013, thanks in part to information provided by an un-indicted mole. This seventh person, according to a criminal complaint, was involved a conversation with Cohen and followed by the selling of $700 million in holdings of two drug companies. This sale took place just one day before a negative drug-trial announcement was announced. Draw your own conclusion on this.

When criminals rip off the money markets for their own gratification or in some cases for playing the big shot role to their friends, it is not just about the money that *they* have illicitly made. It is also, about the money that *others* either do not make or actually loose as a result of that action.

Executive Misbehavior

In separate GSG cases with judges, lawmakers, and regulators, it has been suggested that the bank ignored their conflicts of interest and sold investment to its clients that it knew are weak, all in the pursuit of profit. In 2012 in a very public resignation, one of their bankers in London wrote an op-ed article for the New York Times saying that the GSG sells financial products "that they are trying to get rid of". He went on to remark that "It makes me ill how callously people talk about ripping off their clients".

While we are on the subject of ripping off. Morgan Stanley (MS) had been sued by the American Civil Liberties Union (ACLU) for violating the civil rights laws by encouraging a lender, New Century Mortgage Corp (NCMC), to push risky loans in the black neighborhoods of Detroit. The ACLU and others filed the lawsuit on behalf of the homeowners who took out these loans from NCMC. That corporation was a sub-prime lender which has since gone out of business. The lawsuit claims the MS pushed NCMC to make risky loans because MS took a profit at the start of each loan process, and then sold the loans before they could go bad. That left others who were down the derivatives line holding the bag. As you may know, many of these bad loans ended up in Fanny May and Freddie Mac portfolios, which are insured by the federal government (i.e. us).

How Are You Doin'?

Just how much was or will-be your retirement settlement worth? $250.000? Nothing at all?

Perhaps you are in the wrong business. The place to be is in large corporation management. Apparently there is a: you pad my wallet and I'll pad yours scheme in play at the expense of stockholders and employees. Boards of Directors are aware that the more money they bestow in executive compensation, the more that they are likely to receive for their limited duties. As an example of the limited part, Condoleezza Rice was able to both head up the US State Department and remain on an oil company board at the same time, thereby demonstrating how little work may be required of such figurehead directors. And if she was not devoting sufficient time to her board duties, what do you suspect that she might be getting paid for by the company? Do I need to spell it out?

There is also, a system in place where some executives go from corporate positions, to consultant, to director, to government, to corporate positions, and they benefit from these round-robin journeys because they are very good to others (reciprocity in action) in their fraternity. Not to mention, they can collect multiple (double dip) paychecks.

These connections may not be a subject that is publicly spoken of, but the players have learned how this corrupt system works. As for the executives, how could there be any other rational explanation for their inflated pay other than reciprocity? Certainly, it would not be that they deserve it. So, when one in this exclusive club benefits, they all benefit. I am not aware of a board member ever being confronted, dismissed or prosecuted for conflict-of-interest or fiduciary infidelity.

This high-level fleecing of companies occurs when stockholders don't make the connection between management rip-offs and their lower dividends and stock prices. Shareholders with very large portfolios may also, be part of the problem when they do nothing to correct the situation with their voting rights. This arrangement is somewhat analogous to what happened in the small city in California where the city managers voted themselves and their college's outrageous salaries for doing very little work on the city's behalf. They were, however, busy putting their friends and relatives on the payroll for non-existent jobs.

Another aspect of executive pay revolves around their impressive perks. Personal travel for these people on corporate jets has become commonplace… and not just for the execs, but for the directors that approve this expense as well. A shareholder of Chesapeake Energy Corp. has accused that company of understating the cost of personal travel on their fleet of jets by as much as $10 million per year. The suit alleges that there has been substantial use of this perk, along with the circumvention of public reporting rules. Aircraft expenditures are generally calculated on variable costs such as fuel. They exclude the fixed costs like pilot salaries, maintenance, and the cost of the aircraft. Wouldn't you like to take your next vacation on luxury jet and only pay for your portion of the fuel that is consumed?

The shareholder suit also, alleges that the amount of personal travel involves such a "high proportion of the total use" that the fixed costs should be included in their compensation reporting. The fact that variable costs at this company do not count is an outrage to all shareholders. Do we need any more evidence that the company directors and executives have a cozy arrangement when it comes to benefits?

The wealthy make the regulations that benefit the wealthy - Is this coming as a newsflash to you?

How much are we talking about in excessive executive compensation anyway? An example would be the Home Depot's (HD) golden parachute to a relatively short-term CEO. According to the news reports, after just six years of mediocre performance and much grumbling from the stockholders, he abruptly quit(?). As a result, his severance package was $210.000.000. That's hundreds of millions of dollars folks. Can you imagine what they might have paid him for doing a good job? It is hard to believe that a company even as large as HD would not miss that kind of money. I'm sure the stockholders and lower paid employees would if they could do something about it.

This same executive has taken the helm of another large company, presumably with another extravagant severance package. And that is far from being an isolated example of excess. Packages that are in the hundreds of millions of dollars are more common than you might think. I read about one that was somewhere north of $400.000.000. That is more than $1.000 per day in the average person's lifespan, seven days a week, diapers to diapers.

But not every CEO who is terminated is treated quite So, Well, (a bit of sarcasm). In 2011 Sara Lee Corporation dumped its chief with a pay package valued at only $11.000.000. That is not all that shabby for being fired. If you were let go from your job, you might not even qualify to collect unemployment insurance.

Then there were the unceremonious departures of the CEOs of Fanny Mae and Freddy Mack in 2008 who were also, given golden parachutes. Despite their corporations being deeply involved in the packaging (reselling to investors) of high-risk home mortgage loans, these two received over $30.000.000 in severance pay. That's a nice reward for running their businesses into the ground to the point where they required massive government bailouts.

A survey in 2011 by the Public Affairs Council found that the public had a good opinion of business in general but not of its leadership. And this is even when there are very few people who are intimately aware of the extent of good ol' boy networks and how corrupt the executive compensation is in these exclusive clubs.

Delaware Connection

It turns out that there is a third component in influencing executive pay, and that happens to be the state of Delaware. In return for the revenue that it receives from the incorporations of large businesses, the state's laws and regulations (according to a statement made by Carl Ichan) coddle the directors that coddle the executives with their excessive salaries, bonuses and golden parachutes. Delaware also, makes it illegal for shareholders to bring a legal action that would move a corporation out of the state. So, for their pieces of silver, Delaware allows the unhealthy director-executive connection to function unfettered against the interests of the employees and shareholders. This state qualifies as the same type of venue (flag) shopping that is done by foreign shipping companies So, that they are not subjected to stricter US rules.

According to a survey, more than 60% of the population believes that the rich are responsible for creating wealth and jobs in this country... apparently ignoring the fact that the middle class has been shrinking for years while the upper class is becoming ever more wealthy. And this percentage of poorly informed, true believers has not deviated significantly in the many decades since the original polling on this subject. So, the propaganda that is espoused by the rich has been thoroughly effective. The rest of us just can't seem to get with a rational blame-game to account for people's shrinking income.

Most of us don't even pay due diligence to those billionaires who freely admit that their class is grossly under taxed. In the meantime, the sheep are led to the slaughter, and they go along willingly.

Class Warfare
Not everyone goes to the slaughter quite So, willingly. In recent years there have been street demonstrations in San Francisco by the people who were being evicted from their rentals and by their supporters. These forced move-outs were initiated in order to make expensive upgrades to accommodate the wallets of the nuevo-riche, like those who may have had their fortunes made in Silicon Valley startups. The hikes in rental prices

were driving longtime residents out in order for them to find more affordable digs.

The narrator of this particular TV story said something like 'it is ok for the rich to get richer as long as the middle class does not stagnate'. Well, where did this pin head get his economic education and news from? We have tolerated years of shrinking income for the middle class. And where does he think the money for getting richer comes from? I don't think they print it. A good deal of it comes from those outrageous tax breaks for the wealthy and from executive income and benefits. The stock options for participants in a new business, if that is the case, come at the expense others who may then own a diluted piece of the company.

Maybe it is about time for class warfare to take hold before there is no middle class with enough clout to make a difference.

Competition Reduction

If a company is limited in the prices it can charge the public due to competition and is therefore limited in the profits it can make, the solution sometimes lies in eliminating their competition. No, not like what Standard Oil did in the early days of automobiles when it…
* reduce the price of fuel in locations where there were other gas stations until that competition went out of business

* then raise their prices where they had eliminated the competition to make up for the losses

Today the answer is to buy out the competition with stock, like smaller Air West's attempt to buy out larger Delta Airlines or US Air's proceedings to buy out American.

Here is one formula. First, make an offer to issue stock to cover the cost of to-be purchased company. One might think that this dilution of a company's stock might serve to distress the investors, but not always. What the buying company and its stockholders receive is the other company and its stock, So, the acquiring company's stock is not really watered down. After the purchase occurs, which results in less competition in their field, the acquiring company is in a better position to do things such as…
* terminate or lay off redundant employees
* raise prices with less concern because of diminished competition
* acquire the other company's technology and brain trust
* reduce worker's health or retirement plans if appropriate
* increase profits through economies of scale

The consequence for the consumer can be higher prices and reduced innovation. Reduction in business competition is seldom good for the consumer or the economy.

Oversight Reduction

We should be aware that professional groups such as doctors, veterinarians, lawyers, real estate agents, appraisers, etc. are allowed to establish their own oversight committees which function as judge and jury over their members. When a member violates some guideline, sanctions can be applied. So, far, So, good you say? What you may not be aware of is that these societies are self-governing for the purpose of protecting themselves against government regulations and the public. They can then set up guidelines to limit members of their professions from…
* being witnesses against each other
* contradicting each other
* counseling each another's clients/patients

Because of self-regulation these societies can act as good-ol'-boy networks which then can work against the interests of those who utilize their professional services. It also, means that the members can be subject to the whims of the controlling bodies without an appeal through normal civil channels. Can you imagine what the building industry would be like if its contractors were allowed to police themselves? Fortunately, they are not a society that can afford lobbyists.

Because the aforementioned groups are generally white collar, organized, and have beau coup money for those lobbyists, they have been granted special privileges from the government that others are not So, fortunate to receive. While this is not always a bad thing, it can and does lead to abuse. Without going into detail, when we looked into using a veterinarian oversight committee to sanction a vet for malpractice (nearly causing the death of a pet), we discovered just how uncooperative and protective of their group they can be. The same was true, of course, for the vet's insurance company. So, rather than either of these groups protecting the pet owner, they protected the doctor.

White Collar Crime

More on how we under prosecute white collar businesspersons when they commit non-violent felonies. This is a problem that is not always recognized by the-world-according-to-Republicans who may foolishly believe that businesses are self-regulating.

The numerous complaints that had been made to the Security and Exchange Commission (SEC) about the Madoff scam, for example, had fallen repeatedly on deaf ears. And now that this affair has come to light, where are his co-conspirators? Can one man really steal over fifty billion dollars and not have help from dozens of others?

Investment bankers who created the real estate house-of-cards passed on their derivative's risk, eventually to Fanny May, Freddie Mac and others. This con may have been a low risk/high profit scheme for the bankers, but it created extreme hardships for the millions of homeowners who...
* shouldn't have been qualified for loans in the first place
* lost their homes
* lost equity in their mortgages
* subsequently damaged the housing market

To date none of these traders has yet to pay back a penny of their ill-gotten commissions, which in some cases ran in the hundreds of millions of dollars. Just let Joe blue collar and try to shoplift a shirt at a department store and stay out of jail. We put our foot down on that kind of behavior.

White Collar Stupid

In 2010, 29 men were killed in the worst US coal mining disaster in decades at the Upper Big Branch mine in West Virginia. In 2011 a jury found the security chief guilty of lying to the investigators who were probing that explosion. He was also, found guilty of the disposal of thousands of security-related documents at the Massey Energy Company mine. So, rather than being a help with the investigation, he earned a date with a sentencing hearing.

In 2010 the Gulf of Mexico experienced the world's worst oil spill. It substantially exceeded that of the Exxon Valdez in 1989 which ran aground (thanks to an inattentive captain). BP, the owners of the drilling rig that failed, has been rightly accused of several well-duhs when they...
* drilled far below the 18.000-foot depth that was permitted
* had not installed the blowout prevention device that should have been located 200 feet in the seabed (they reportedly saved about $50.000 by skipping this device)
* installed only one switch that could stop the oil flow, and that may have been located where the explosion occurred, leaving the remaining crew with no options
* tried to encourage the fishermen who were voluntarily helping in the containment to sign waivers of liability against BP should something go wrong
* made an effort to lay the blame for the spill on the company that operated the rig
* claimed that their liability was limited, after endlessly repeating that they would take full responsibility for the spill

Thanks to Vice President Chaney's assurance years earlier (you may recall that he and President Bush came from the oil industry), the oil companies were guaranteed that their blowout liability would be limited to $75 million... an incredibly tiny amount when compared to the Gulf of Mexico's cleanup price tag that ran into the billions of dollars or compared to BP's $5.6 billion profit for the quarter in which the spill occurred.

It should come as no surprise to anyone that major companies would play fast and loose with their liability. Corporate America's first responses to misdeeds are denial and subterfuge. It does not much matter that it was BP which was the responsible party in this particular case. Other large corporation might have pursued the same course of action.

Business integrity revolves around the bottom line for the executives and shareholders (which include the executives). On top of this tragedy, you have the deep-thinker Rush Limbaugh taking sides with BP. I wonder if that was because he is also, big business and empathizes with others in that class.

By mid-2011 only a few billion of the $20 billion cleanup funds had been allocated to those who suffered damages. On the other hand, the law office of Kenneth Fienberg was receiving $15 million per year to oversee BP's disbursements while the victims struggled to receive any or full compensation in time to save their businesses. I would have done Fienberg's job for a whole lot less. All along, BP was repeatedly feeding us the propaganda that they were doing all that they could to help those in need.

On the surface it seems like Fienberg's concerns for the little guys also, appears to be minimal. Or perhaps it is just one more situation where big business gets special breaks from those who are part of or sympathetic to big business.

In 2012 BP began a major ad campaign telling us how Well, the clean-up and recovery of businesses the Gulf States was taking place. No real examples, just blather. And the press seemed to be in no great hurry to dispute the claims. So, in the subsequent years we should believe that everything is getting back to normal. Sure.

Undeserved Credit

It has taken years to overcome the technological problems and business reluctance required to begin producing a low sulfur diesel fuel. As frequently happens, Europe is ahead of us in the areas of conservation and pollution control because they do not permit the oil companies to dictate policies to them… as least not as much as we do. They are concerned with the environmental impact of excessive use of fuels.

But as soon as the mandated European-style reformulation of the fuel for cars sold in Europe was completed in the US, the oil industry creatives were prepared with their self-promoting ads that took credit for this achievement. There is just no hint of integrity with the oil companies because their oligopoly status insures that there can be a lack of veracity and responsibility to the consumer.

Deserved Discredit

While most of us believe that there is sufficient evidence to support the CO2 connection to global warming, there is a minority that is still intent on debunking that theory about the cause of the current warming trend. Among them is a major oil company which has for years funded a company-line think tank dealing with this subject. In their efforts to distract the public from the peril, they offered a fee to any author that could make (make-up?) a case against the idea that global warming is man-made.

The industry's attempt to deter the public from the notion of our planet being in environmental jeopardy is similar to the tobacco industry's campaign in the 1980's of trying to convince us that their products were not hazardous to our health. You may remember that each tobacco CEO swore under oath before Congress that they were unaware of any credible connection to cancer and other health concerns. This level of deceit is now being practiced by big oil with their employing several of the tobacco industry's techniques, such as…

* funneling money to sympathetic Congresspersons who have no integrity (I guess that covers just about all of them)
* engaging in disingenuous and attention diverting advertising
* providing financial support for disinformation articles and speakers that pretend to be unbiased
* sowing doubt wherever possible

The problem with consumers is that their apathy toward self-education lends them to being easily manipulated. Listening to what experts say rather than paying attention to conscienceless promoters and politicians is not high on peoples wavelength.

Invasion of Privacy

Many Americans take for granted that we have the legal protection against the invasion of personal privacy. They might be surprised to learn that the Constitution offers no such specific assurances. Yes, the framers did include a Bill of Rights with related provisions in this area. Among them are...
* privacy of beliefs (1st Amendment)
* privacy of a home against demands that it be used to house soldiers (3rd Amendment)
* privacy of a person and possessions against unreasonable searches (4th Amendment)

* privacy of personally held information... aka the privilege against self-incrimination (5th Amendment)

As for this last amendment, we may mistakenly construe that our personal information has been protected by the force of law. Nothing could be further from the truth. While no one can compel us to reveal our secrets (except by granting immunity or in some cases, the threat of contempt), this is exactly what we do voluntarily on a routine basis.

Public revelations can come about when our personal transactions take place in the public domain, such as through banking, borrowing, purchasing, using the courts, and the Internet. And nearly all of this data is recorded by companies who make our information their own business in order to sell that data to interested parties, including the government.

These data capturing companies maintain records on virtually all of us, and their databases include the billions of transactions that take place and are recorded in the public domain. It is collected, collated, and served up to the buyers who may glean, among other things, what are our...
* home address and phone numbers
* religious preferences
* buying habits

* mortgage debt
* family structure
* court history
* individual and family income
* offenses that we may have committed

Ever since George Orwell's classic book dealing with the perils of big brother government there have been the occasional, dire warnings from a handful of citizens as to the adverse consequences of having power concentrated in the hands of a few. For years we have been warned of this encroachment into our private lives, and the warnings have gone mostly unheeded.

Sure, there are a number of fringe groups that extol the evils of the state, but they too are largely ignored. That is unless they address their grievances with violent or illegal action. With their paranoia comes the imagined repression which serves to fuel their extremist beliefs. Need I mention the initials NRA as a dedicated group loosely falling into this mindset?

Who would have thought that it would be businesses and Internet criminals, rather than our government, who are leading the assault on our being left to live in peace and quiet? Forget for the moment the malicious hackers who inflict harm for their monetary advantage. Business spam and click-tracking on the Internet are pervasive, and it is trending ever more in that direction. When you browse on the net there is software that wants to know what you are buying and what your surfing habits are in order to target you for future invasions.

When I joined the Air Force many years ago I was surprised to learn that they were aware of a traffic ticket that I had received. Now if this information could be So, easily obtained by some entity before mass computerization, what do you think today's snooping capabilities are?

A big-brother exposé revealed that Google has kept a record of every inquiry ever made by every person who has ever used their search engine. While they claim that they have no nefarious motive for this failure to delete, they are not spending millions of dollars on data storage for nothing. It is only a matter of time before they decide to sell this data to those companies who will use it to pigeonhole our activities for whatever motives they might have. And the folks at Google had the brass to lobby (successfully) to have their company excluded from a privacy protection law.

In 2011 MasterCard and Visa announced their intentions to tie their vast databases of credit card purchases to each cardholder's online experiences for the purpose of targeted advertising. These product connections would then be sold to companies So, that they could provide ads that may reflect our interests. For example, if you subscribed to an automobile magazine, you might be subjected to receiving car ads on your browser. While the details of this new form of database mining had not been worked out as of this writing, the handwriting is on the wall.

Back in 2011 Fair Isaac (the folks who brought us the FICO credit scoring) announced that they are branching out into the new area (for them) that involves the understanding of human behaviors. This is not an intellectual quest, but rather it is being done to determine the ways to predict our actions in order to sell that information to those companies which will use it to their own advantage.

I suppose there are some who will not consider these probes into our lives to be much of an invasion of privacy. Perhaps they can even be viewed as being an improvement on the annoying, pointless ads we are now inundated with. Count me out on that score.

Invasion By Software

When I receive an offer to upgrade an installed piece of freeware I wonder how much of the new coding is devoted to improving the product and how much of it is directed at nagware (those popup solicitations to upgrade to a pro version, or worse). One piece of anti-malware had reverted to issuing several-times-daily nags about upgrading, in contrast to their previous monthly or the-computer-has-been-rebooted schedule.

Another piece of freeware (Ad-Aware) repeatedly tried to install a toolbar even after I un-clicked the box to permit it. When this toolbar popup failed to go away I uninstalled the software. When that did not get rid of the nagware, another piece of software that I use came on the screen telling me how to rid the computer of this persisting annoyance. Fortunately, my computer background allowed me to understand and follow their technical instructions and clear the last remnants of the software. I imagine that other, less trained users just go nuts.

With some so-called helpware software, the cure can be worse than the original problem.

If one is not circumspect about paying close attention to each new version during its installation, it may download an unwanted toolbar, change your browser's home page, change your browser, or add other pieces of software that are either unwanted or unsafe.

More than once, I have had to uninstall offending software to rid my computer from attached nuisanceware. Sometime the software is embedded So, deeply into the computer's innards that highly specialized products are required to get the job done. Fortunately for me, I have thirty plus years of dealing with computer ills to fall back on. My sympathies to those who don't. Still, once in every few years or so I have to completely flush the computer, reinstall the operating system, and then reinstall all of my software to get back to normal… a very time-consuming process.

After updating one freeware product I immediately began receiving junk mail that continued in spite of reporting it to a government site. Trying to unsubscribe to these senders of garbage only serves to guarantee that you will receive even more junk mail in the future because you have now verified your email address to the bad guys. This well-intended but pointless action may result in having your address sold to other bad guys.

If you are receiving a lot of junk email and your browser has an auto-block option, that feature can be useful feature. If not, your best option may be to abandon the old address and create a new one. Hopefully your contact list is up to date So, that you can notify one and all about the change.

I received a series of no subject emails from a neighbor, which I immediately deleted. Later he sent out a warning message to those in his address book that he had been hacked. My reply to him (as politely as I could) was that this problem occurred due to some action he had taken, and that he may want to home in on the cause So, as to not have it happen again. It is less likely that his situation came about because of someone else's poor computer judgment, a stolen email list is one for example, but that is always possible.

As I have advocated forever, never click on any links at unknown web sites or on links of any kind sent to you by friends. The chances of infecting your computer with this action are substantial. The only exception to this rule might be an attachment that you know was created by the sender… such as photos. But even then you can never be positive of the contents without contacting the sender in advance of opening.

Those of us who buy books at traditional shops do expect anonymity from those interests who may want to profile us. But this is turning out not to be the case with the increasingly popular downloaded ebooks. The purveyors have our email addresses and selection tastes to use as they see fit because the government has yet to protect us with any meaningful extension to privacy laws.

Now it is unlikely in the extreme that information about the sales of these ebooks will be used in a seriously nefarious way. However, it will certainly contribute to the flood of spam that reaches inboxes or with the ads that pop up on browsers. Then it is only a matter of time before the data is marketed to others for their own purposes, just like our public records now are. Computers have the capacity to store and collate zillions of pieces of information, and they are being used for that exact purpose.

Of course, we have all read-about/heard-about the profusion of identity theft cases. By now we should all know about shredding our documents rather than just trashing them. In spite of this there are millions who want every detail of their lives broadcast over the social networks. Undoubtedly this is because of the mild brain high that I mentioned earlier. But no good act goes unpunished. The bad guys have taken to extracting and using this inside information to impersonate the blather-er to their elderly relatives, using horror stories about their needing emergency money. Then they asked to have the money sent ASAP before the story can be verified.

HOW POLITICS FAILS US

What We Should Know About the People Running Our Government.

Table Of Contents

Introduction

Definition of politics: Ideology where real world consequences and truth take a back seat to personal prejudices and compromise.

I suppose politics has always been a dirty game, played by those with power to gain and little substance to offer their constituents. It's not that they don't have the skill set to provide positive guidance and civic improvements for the rest of us. It's more likely that they lack the incentive to fight the system that they become ensconced in. After all, it provides them with a level of benefits that you and I could only hope for. Short of running for reelection, there is so little work to do, and being productive in the law-making process is not a target.

Samuel Clements, writer & humorist: *"Imagine that you are an idiot. Then imagine that you are a member of Congress... wait, I repeat myself"*

Participation in government has been structured to provide a degree of luxury and job security far beyond that which is deserved by the participants. A self-serving seniority system has been developed that allows those who take up the top rungs of the ladder to exercise enormous control over those who are situated below them. Equality among Congresspersons is merely a figment of the imagination of those who are without a clue. As a result of this structure, little gets done that does not play into the quest for power by those at the top.

I suppose it is natural that being in the 'public service' with all of its heady perks would give any ordinary person a terrific ego boost. The problem, however, arises when one's ego becomes larger than one's brain. Invariably what we end up with, much like that which occurs some business environments, are candidates who are mostly being voted into their level of incompetence.

Plato, philosopher: "One of the penalties for refusing to participate in politics is that you end up being governed by your inferiors."

So, do I feel that government is essentially corrupt and without any redeeming value? Not Completely. If the politicians were thoroughly worthless, this country would not occupy the position that it holds on the world's stage. It is just that they could do better... as a matter of fact, considerably better. But then that would require raking over the coals the power system that makes them So, very comfortable and So, very unresponsive to the people's interests. It would mean giving up the easy reelection money with the incumbent obligations that come from the loose purse-strings of big business. Fat chance.

It has been said that politicians are interested in four 'P' things - Power, Perks, Pork and the polite version, Privates.

From My Perspective

My definition of politics: Ideology where real world consequences and truth take a back seat to personal prejudices and corruption.

I suppose politics has always been a dirty game, played by those with power to gain and little substance to offer their constituents. It's not that they don't have the skill set to provide positive guidance and civic improvements for the rest of us. It's more likely that they lack the incentive to fight the system that they become ensconced in. After all, it provides them with a level of benefits that you and I could only hope for. Short of running for reelection, there is so little work to do, and being productive in the law-making process is not an ambition.

Samuel Clements, writer & humorist: "Imagine that you are an idiot. Then imagine that you are a member of Congress... wait, I repeat myself"

Participation in government has been structured to provide a degree of luxury and job security far beyond that which is deserved by the participants. A corrupt, self-serving, seniority system has been developed that allows those who take up the top rungs of the ladder to exercise enormous control over those who are situated below them. Equality among Congresspersons is merely a figment of the imagination of those who are without a clue. As a result of this structure, little gets done that does not play into the quest for power by those at the top.

I suppose it is natural that being in the public service with all of its heady perks would give any ordinary person a terrific ego boost. The problem, however, arises when one's ego becomes larger than one's brain. Invariably what we end up with, much like that which occurs some business environments, are candidates who are mostly being voted into their level of incompetence.

Plato, philosopher: "One of the penalties for refusing to participate in politics is that you end up being governed by your inferiors."

So, do I feel that government is essentially corrupt and without any redeeming value? Not Completely. If the politicians were thoroughly worthless, this country would not occupy the position that it holds on the world's stage. It is just that they could do better... as a matter of fact, immensely better. But then that would require raking over the coals the power system that makes them So very comfortable and so very unresponsive to the people's interests. It would mean giving up the easy reelection money with the incumbent obligations that come from the loose purse-strings of big business. Fat chance.

It has been said that politicians are interested in the four P things - Power, Perks, Pork, and (the polite version) Privates.

The 2-Party System

'System' is an appropriate descriptor for the manner in which politics is pursued in America. It permits candidates to start with a roughly fifty-fifty chance of being elected to office, which is not too bad for persons who have few qualifications beyond oratory. After that the system takes over. And unless they seriously screw up once they are in office, they are in like Flynn.

The logic that for some justifies our outmoded electoral process may be that a time and money-consuming, three-party, run-off is not required. The person with the most votes is not forced to negotiate a platform with multiple parties, as is the case with other countries.

A downside to this method of selection is that party platforms become inflexible since money flows to those platform positions that are of interest to big business. In other words, party positions become rigid to avert an interruption in their campaign financing. The result is that important issues may have little chance of receiving or surviving a fair hearing.

So, what is this fixation that voters have with party affiliations anyway? Am I missing something important here? Is one side mostly mistaken with their particular platform while the other side is mostly correct with theirs? Is it the herd instinct in play?

Friedrich Nietzsche, philosopher: "Insanity in individuals is rare - but in groups, parties, nations, and epochs it is the rule."

To top off this unrealistic must-go-with-a-party mind frame, some states require voters to sign a party-designated registration prior to voting. Then there is the ill-conceived but foolishly convenient option of voting a straight party ticket, which only perpetuates the: its-my-party silliness. Why should people vote for a gaggle of candidates that they are not familiar with on poorly thought-out philosophical grounds? Why should we believe in a black and white political world when life is cast in shades of grey? How did we become to be So, myopically one-sided in the first place? Well, perhaps it is the herd instinct.

Mark Russell, humorist: "You've got the brainwashed, that's the Democrats, and the brain-dead, that's the Republicans!"

Bill O'Reilly of Fox News said surprisingly to his credit during the 2008 campaign that he did not care much about the individual parties. He just wanted to know the politician's positions on the issues. I can just hear some witless voter saying, "But you can't have positions without having parties".

Unfortunately, both sides in the political game are, as usual, short on specifics and long on pandering platitudes and disingenuous sound bites. Getting away with this self-serving, anti-voter-interest conduct can be partially attributed to people's lack of ability to assess what is being told to them. If one is continually being deceived by irrelevant arguments, who is at fault…those who are the liars or those who allow themselves to be lied to?

George Orwell, author: *"In a time of universal deceit, telling the truth is a revolutionary act."*

I was at a luncheon when one of my friends pulled out a local absentee ballot and asked others at the table if they knew some of the people on the ballot. One attendee wondered if this ballot was for just one of the parties. The answer was Yes. Apparently my friend had no fondness for anyone from the other party or their platforms.

Shouldn't we consider that both parties have a few decent ideas to offer and more than a few ideas to reproach? So, why is it that So, many of us are adamant about supporting a single party of their choice? I can account for a few possibilities in support of this peculiar behavior. It may be that people...

* became interested in a particular party as children when their acceptance level was high - a form of indoctrination

* grew up in an environment (rich or poor) and related to those interests and the party that was most intimately linked to their pocketbook - a form of it's all about me

* became involved with a party that was popular with their social group or their campus mates - a form of follow the leader

* they researched the differences between all of the candidates and made informed judgments - a rare form of intelligence

What are the chances that the last possibility is the one that leads to most people's party affiliation? Slim to none I expect. If even a small amount of due diligence were involved in approaching party-choice decisions it would be impossible to align oneself with a single party on all issues. Being an independent that decides matters on their merits makes more sense. But then we do not always use this logic and common sense as our guide to forming opinions. Mostly we are persuaded by influences (good and bad) that we encounter around us and find enticing.

James Bovard, Civil Libertarian: *"Democracy must be something more than two wolves and a sheep voting on what to have for dinner."*

On the positive side, in 2011 it was reported that 40% of us now consider themselves to be Independents. This is a far cry from the 10% of just a few decades ago when only loony bins were So, inclined. It shows a significant disaffection with the polarization that has been shamelessly demonstrated by both parties.

In 2012 the satisfaction level with federal politicians was reported to be a measly 9 percent. The decades of political nonsense may finally be coming home to roost, but I wouldn't hold my breath. I suspect it will be many years before the politicians truly get the message from a mostly silent electorate.

On the Larry King show in 2010, Jesse Ventura, ex-professional wrestler and ex-governor of Minnesota, suggested that the main problem with the politics is that we are "subjected to the Republicans and the Democrats". He went on to say that their staged antipathy toward each other is accounted for by two things. They...
* are phony, like professional wrestling (politicians do socialize in private)
* act against the best interests of the country (by putting their own interests first)

John Adams, President: *"In my many years I have come to a conclusion that one useless man is a shame, two is a law firm, and three or more is a congress."*

Mother of Deception

There are beliefs that can be beneficial, and there are those that work against our welfare. One of the more counterproductive ideas is that our country is being governed by the politicians for the benefit of their constituents. Even a cursory examination of their political behaviors and lack of effective governing should make these failures evident to all but the most indoctrinated or disinterested.

The reality is that our political leadership has long since given up their autonomy to the interests of major corporations and their collection of lobbyists with deep pockets. How these politicians vote on any issue has been subjugated to a desire to be reelected to office. This means accepting whatever campaign funding that they can lay their hands on, regardless of the attached strings. Knowing this fact about politics, corporations willingly subsidize the reelection efforts with contributions to both parties, while at the same time exacting a toll of loyalty. Could their making political payments to both sides be any more telling about their motives?

Political decisions, policies, and laws are not being made based on concerns for the interests of the public. If that were the case we would not be...
* the last industrialized country without an decent healthcare system
* encouraged to buy massive SUVs and trucks for routine use
* traveling to Canada or Mexico to purchase drugs and healthcare at reduced prices
* constantly being misled by a flood of false advertising, which now occupies about one third

of television viewing time thanks to deregulation years ago (early regulations permitted stations to have only six minutes of commercials per hour)
* wondering why there is so much cancer, while at the same time eating contaminated foods and permitting corporations to pollute the environment
* thinking about the cost of school lunches rather than being concerned with their nutritional content
* spending billions on wars in countries that are not worth saving because it suits our military-industrial-complex
* having our citizen's interests systematically subverted to those of big oil, big drugs, big banks, big insurance, etc.

Does anyone think a $40 billion profit in one year by Exxon is even remotely reasonable? That is more than $100 for every man, woman and child living in America, or about $400 per average family that is bestowed on just one of the big oil interests.

Becoming a Lobbyist

Going back to lobbyists for a bit, just who are these people anyway, and how can they exercise power over the political process. Well, I am not aware of any college offering a course or degree in this profession. That means that the skill has to be learned on the job. I am also, not aware that there are openings advertised in the want ads for such wannabe candidates. What that means is that these people have to be self-promoted into the occupation.

Ok, how does that fortuitous situation come about? It starts by their getting to know people in positions of power. And what better way is there than to be a sitting member of Congress or a high placed staff member of such a person. In addition to one's official duties, learning who is who and who is not becomes a valuable trade. And trade is an appropriate descriptor since being successful in this field requires the ability and resources to do horse trading. Quite often that means trading perks for votes.

Lobbyists, contrary to the opinion of the uninformed, do not go before Congress just to present a company's viewpoint. Their job is to promote that viewpoint by whatever means may be at their disposal. As a rule, that task involves applying whatever pressure they can bring to bear to help Congresspersons see the light.

So, congress, in an effort to be all things to all people (except for the voters), goes along with the flow which can push them up-stream toward reelection. And when it is their turn to retire from office, there are ready jobs for many of the politicians, staffers, and department heads who found it future-convenient to cooperate with business's who sought out their favors. And not So, surprisingly, they are offered those jobs that sometimes involve becoming a lobbyist or executives. So, lobbyists, Congresspersons, and corporate executives have a nice round-robin club going for themselves.

Changing Landscapes

When I was younger, the makeup of political parties ran along liberal and conservative fiscal lines. The questions were...
* who paid for what - federal or state
* who had the authority - federal or state
* how much legislation should be directed toward or against business
* how much welfare would be doled out to the needy
* how much social security should be returned to the retired
* how much power should unions hold
* how big or small should government be
* what industries should we subsidize, if any
* do we bail out large companies that get in trouble
* do we balance the federal budget

The Republican Party was generally known to be on the side of smaller government and bigger business, while rarely throwing a bone to the poor. The Democratic Party was in favor of

tossing money at problems rather than coming up with real solutions. Since those happy days…
* both parties have joined the race to see how much spending they can get away with because it suits their reelection efforts
* Bill Clinton, for example, took as many issues away from the Republicans as he could - regardless of his actual political heritage or beliefs
* Carl Rove did the same for Bush by accusing the Democrats of the same issues that were Republican's weak suits
* political pork projects have gotten even more out of control - like the multi-million-dollar bridge to nowhere in Alaska just to make Senator Ted Stevens look good to his constituents - which was subsequently cancelled by then Governor Palin, who then kept the funds in Alaska anyway.

In Recent years a change of political behavior became very clear. Republicans, having been hurt by their minority status, decided that just say "no" was more than an anti-drug philosophy. It became their marching song.

Another of their platforms has been the promotion of religious dogma by conservatives who can't seem to mind their own business. When Jack Kennedy, a Catholic, ran for President, he promised that religion would not influence his political judgments. When George Romney, a Mormon, ran for President he made essentially the same pledge. Their religious preferences were a private matter and were not up for consideration as public policy.

Today the advocates for religion have once again come out of the closet, predominately filling the ranks of the Republican Party. They work to inflict their views on legislation at all levels of government. I suspect that resorting to a theocracy (God based government) would be the culmination of their dreams. Just look how Well, that has worked out for the Muslims.

The problem with merging church and state in government is the intolerance factor. Faith-based advocates are generally not the live-and-let-live types with a gentle agenda. They would happily put the force of law behind their rigid mindsets and move the rest of us into lockstep with their obsessive need to promote religious concepts.

Making abortions illegal would presumably be high on their targets of opportunity. Even if that particular issue is of no consequence to you, there could be other dictates to impinge on your rights and freedoms. And to what good end, if any? The world has never been Well, served when religion controlled the helm of a government.

As for the intolerance issue, perhaps minding one's own business would not be a bad starting point, as opposed to the relentless march toward a follow-the-leader mentality. No one has a lock on right and wrong, and no one should be allowed to promote their religious focus through the force of law.

To be fair and balanced politically, the Democrats have their share of radicals among their ranks as well. The main difference is that they seem to be more people-problems-to-excess oriented rather than their counterpart's business-profits-to-excess oriented. Being people oriented is directed towards getting votes. Being business oriented is directed towards re-election funding.

Regardless, this does not excuse either side from *any* extreme viewpoint. We need to reject extremism and instill tolerance, conciliation, and compromise as the appropriate model for problem resolution and social advancement. The only alternative to this is a continuing, unnecessary, state of contrived strife among politicians with little legislative progress to show for it.

In recent elections the Democrats have come up with a devious plan for retaining office. They buy votes. Illegal you say? Perhaps So, technically, but not in reality. Why do you think So, little has been done to keep out the poor from the Americas to the south? They tend to vote Democratic in support of the dole that is bestowed on them. If you do not see this as buying votes, you have my sympathy for your higher taxes that result.

In 2014 a poll showed that Congress had only a 9 percent approval rating. That's more than nine out of ten who feel that they are not doing a good job. So, one has to wonder how these politicians are immune enough from negative public opinion to continue unfettered with their do-nothing agenda. Well, the answer that I have come up with is that their quest for power blinds them to certain realities. And the herd instinct tells them that all is well… if so-and-So, can do it and get away with it So, can I.

For and Against

As we should all know by now, politicians are consistently against virtually all proposals that are proffered by their opponents. The ugly sport that they play is to bash their adversaries, while at the same time offering little of worth in exchange. This occurs because if one is on record as being in favor of specific ideas they might have more difficulty selling their votes to the lobbyists.

An even darker view of politics is that public display of disagreement on issues is a game of let's pretend which is designed for the public's consumption. It is a manufactured derision that consists of posturing and obstruction. Votes are sometimes taken in the open, but the issues may be decided in the so-called, smoke-filled, back rooms. More often than not it is the most powerful members of Congress and their corporate backers that hold an undeniable sway over the less powerful members.

Does anyone remember when it was that compromise became a four-letter word in government?

The prevailing attitude in congress is that politics is essentially about confrontation and not about compromise. Perhaps newly elected legislators do expect to use negotiation upon arrival in office, but very quickly they learn that the boss-controlled system is alive and well, in Washington. This is the protected environment where those who are at the top of the party ladder dictate their party's voting policy to those members who are on the rungs below them. They are able to accomplish this task because they control advancements, perks, and appointments which lead to...
* being recognized to present bills
* being given better office accommodations

* advancing to more prestigious job positions
* going on travel assignments
* receiving additional pay

The impetus of the senior politicians is to appease the lobbyists and to badmouth the opponents. Give nothing and propose nothing has become the political battle cry. As a result, we have a smokescreen of exaggerated animosity accompanied by very little productivity in Congress. This behavior is shameful beyond words, but few of us are willing to acknowledgement it and demand a change. The natural result of Congress's failure to consider other's points of view is that vital issues may be sidelined or diluted.

In 2011 and 2012 Congress reached its zenith with the squabbling over a budget limit, spending, and taxes. This propensity to avoid these real matters is infamous in government, but somehow that behavior does not lead to embarrassment because So, few of us are objecting to the sideshow.

When he was first elected to office, Governor Schwarzenegger of California failed miserably with initiatives that were directed at changing, as he saw it, the state's outdated policies. This occurred due to his aggressively going up against the entrenched powers, and his doing little to consult with the opposition. It was simply a matter of the terminator in action. But Arnold was a person who could learn a lesson from failure. Eventually he set up a smoking tent where both parties could get together to work out their differences… and with some success. What a novel idea to turn your opposition into your confederate.

Since politics is primarily the business of getting reelected to office, that means defeating one's opponents by any method at one's disposal, using fair play or not. While a responsible voting record should be sufficient to produce these same results for an incumbent, the truth is that voters have virtually no idea what the representatives in their jurisdiction actually stand for or vote for beyond a few sound bites. Some may know what a politician's public pronouncements are, but this is a far cry from their being privy to politician's actions and intentions.

When was the last time you saw a politician's voting record in print? Rarely? Maybe never? Why isn't this information offered to us by the press on a regular basis? On one occasion I read an article about a Governor's complete veto record, which was presented as a measure of her mindset. I was impressed with the details that were presented in print. But this rare reporting was the exception that proves the rule.

Problems With Power

One of the problems with elected officials is that they have developed a system where the longer one is in office, the more power they may accrue for themselves over other members with lesser tenure. To put that into perspective, all Congresspersons are not treated equally when they take their seat of office. For junior legislators, the concept of one-person one-vote is actually one-person no-real-vote. Those have long since been sold to the highest bidder or put under the thumb of the members above them.

This also, means that the Congressional leadership is the major recipient of corporate funding in order to have them promote the corporate interest and policies down through the ranks. In a very public statement in 2011, the Senate Speaker told his conservative colleges to fall in line on a particular fiscal issue or risk losing their plum committee assignment. Enough said? Well, actually not…how dare he!

A possible solution to this corruption of values would be to set term limits for politicians into law. No congressperson could then serve more than two consecutive terms. To be fair to those who are members of the House of

Representative would have their two year terms extended to six years, like the Senator's terms. Should various congresspersons be particularly Well, liked, they could run again after an absence from office.

This change would accomplish several things…
* no congressperson would have more than one incredibly wasteful reelection campaign
* politics would be more inclined toward public service rather than providing themselves with a job haven
* lobbyists would have less incentive to dole money out to congresspersons for their loyalty because they might actually become independent (lame duck) politicians if reelected
* the need to cultivate lobbyists would be So, abated that the congresspersons might actually vote on the citizens behalf
* the powers of congressional leadership would be drastically diminished by virtue of shortened terms and diluted seniority
* it is likely that the cast system, with committee heads holding much of the power, would come to an end

Jesse Ventura, ex-governor of Minnesota: "Politics is the worst business in America."

An acquaintance of mine had an opportunity to travel with a member of Congress on a fact-finding mission, and was stunned to see what a thirst for power that person had…

* kiss-up assistants were at his beck and call
* no request for frivolous service would be turned down
* he ate at the best restaurants, with food and drink prices meaning nothing because they were paid for by the public
* special favors were expected and given wherever he went

So, is it any wonder that these representatives sell their votes So, easily to stay in office? Their attitude of entitlement also, rubs off on the President and his wife. It has been reported that while First Ladies generally had two or three assistants. Michelle is said to retain in the neighborhood of twenty. Dare we say there are visions of royalty dancing through her arrogant head? Of course, there are the frequent, personal trips that the President and his family take at the taxpayer's expense. So, much for his caring who pays for a round of golf at about $1.000.000 a pop.

Edmond Burke, writer: *"The greater the power, the more dangerous the abuse."*

Privilege for the Privileged

When a small-engine plane crashes there may be 1 or 2 investigators normally assigned to look into the case. But this was not the normal situation when the pilot happened to be the son of US Senator Inhofe. The National Transportation Safety Board (NTSB) assigned 7 from the NTSB, 3 from the FAA, and 4 from the plane's various parts manufacturers to study the details of the crash. Anything to try to show that it was not pilot error, which is overwhelmingly the normal case in small plane accidents.

They also, interviewed some 20 others consisting of flight controllers, a flight instructor, and the widow who was asked to detail his eating, sleeping, drinking, and snoring habits. And the money required to pursue this operation was apparently not an object of consideration.

A private plane crash might warrant, under some circumstances, as many as 5 investigators to be involved, but this was not the case with John F. Kennedy Jr. He rated 45. Other celebrities and politicians have also, scored higher than normal with the scrutiny their crashes. I suspect that there may have been substantial pressure brought to bear in those cases as well.

Speaking of Speaking

It is interesting to note when a politician is outraged enough to make an issue of something. It predominantly occurs when they are defending their misbehaviors or are seeking reelection to office in a tight race. The insiders in Washington are of course privy to why this pompous rhetoric takes place. So, Congresspersons apply the appropriate grain of salt to what is being said, even when they are being made a target.

They also, know that their fellow politicians do not ordinarily go out on a limb because they have much to lose. They...
* must first run their ideas past the powers that be, or risk censure if they step outside of the party line (Just look at the Republican pinhead in 2010 that defended BP, and quickly offered the lame apology that he was misunderstood. He had been confronted by the leadership and told to retract his statement or step down from a prized committee post)
* can lose precious bargaining chips that can be bartered with other politicians or lobbyists
* might risk alienating some of their constituents by being candid
* cannot easily deny what they say in public

Remember the line from The Godfather or the advice that Jackie Kennedy-Onassis ostensibly received from her mother? It went something like: Never tell anyone what you are thinking So, they can't use it to your disadvantage. For this and other reasons, politicians rarely express their innermost thoughts unless they are desperately in need of publicity for their home campaigns, committee posts, and when a degree of honesty would benefit them.

Sound Bite Politics

With the advent of huge campaign war chests and frequent access to TV broadcast time, politicians have long since discovered that their seconds-long ads work Well, for them. This politicking technique succeeds because a message can be delivered to the public without the opportunity for return information (criticism). As a result, these nearly valueless sound bites are not challenged as they might be in a debate or community forum.

The consequence of this format is that...
* there is a lack of pertinent information disseminated because image creation, not content, is on the agenda
* opponents are painted with false or negative ads that serve no educational reality, but they may stick in voters' minds when they go to the polls
* issues and platforms are typically ignored in an effort to avoid offending anyone, with platitudes ruling the day
* the press contents itself with news about $400 haircuts, slip-of-the-tongues, and other issues because they are in business of *creating* sensationalism for a scandal-thirsty public

The sound bite politics employed today have several implications in that they...

* show a shameful disrespect for the voter by not delivering real information

* isolate politicians from experiencing or having to responding to contradictory points of view

* permit politicians to imagine that they have an understanding of new bills - which they don't since they may not even read the laws that they vote on

* turn politics into show business

Wrong Side - Again

In 2015 it had been reported in the news that there was a mini movement, once again, to have restaurants and (especially) fast food chains label the nutritional values of their food… and not just the calorie counts. Apparently there are more women and Democrats in support of this issue than there are Republicans, whose mantra has long been: business is self-regulating, and government should stay out of business. Sure, they are. While the Republicans do not have a monopoly on bad judgment, too much political posturing on the part of both parties is supported by the unrestrained corporate bribes at the expense of consumers.

No Where to Turn

Those of us who have an interest in in-depth information about our government's apparatus may be relegated to receiving their political analysis (he says humorously) from comedians like Bill Maher and John Stewart. The problem with this venue is that their guests are predominantly liberal, and they may not have balanced presentations. Don't conservatives have something constructive to say, or even a sense of humor? If you watch people like Hannity of Fox News, humor and fairness can be as ethereal as a light breeze. He's a liberal basher in the extreme, which involves the repetitive voicing of mean-spirited innuendos and falsehoods.

The problem associated with many of the media's talking heads is that they anchor news programs which are populated with biased reporters and guest propagandist who...
* may have no solutions
* might show no insightfulness
* espouse mostly anti-opponent-party lines

When they happen to book opposing point-of-view spokespersons at the same time, the airwaves are filled with...
* annoying childish banter
* irrelevant arguments
* frequently interrupted statements

All of this verbal nonsense may leave voters with the accurate feeling that there is no one listening to them, and that they might have no better choice than to give up on the system. Not so surprisingly this realistic attitude works to the advantage of the incumbent politicians. They are then free to carry out their re-election efforts with minimal scrutiny from voters.

Bill Maher, comedian: "Freedom isn't free. It shouldn't be a bragging point that Oh, I don't get involved in politics, as if that makes someone cleaner. No, that makes you derelict of duty in a republic. Liars and panderers in government would have a much harder time of it if So, many people didn't insist on their right to remain ignorant and blindly agreeable."

When there is the occasional criticism from the press, news editorials, or public protest, it rolls off politicians like the proverbial water off a duck's back. They clearly have more important business to focus on, which may not involve listening to their constituents. So much for having an effective representative-democracy in this country. While the Constitution framers wrote in fairly effective checks and balances on the three branches of government, someone apparently forgot about addressing the non-performance of elected officials. I guess they assumed all would take care of itself.

Coffee or Tea Anyone

In 2009 and 2010 we saw the temporary creation of the ultra-liberal Coffee party and emergence of the ultra-conservative Tea party. The latter came into being as a reaction to two situations... a lack of effective political leadership and the frenzy that was whipped up by the polarizing talking heads. They gave people the impression that they were not being listened to and that Congressional spending was heading the country toward bankruptcy (we should all recall the downgrading of the US's credit rating in the past).

While there may-have-been/may-be something positive to say in regard to both parties' platforms respectively, people have not gotten the idea that voting an incumbent out of office is more effective than blowing off a lot of hot air at town meetings. What better method do we have to send a message to ineffectual Congresspersons than to remove them from office?

Vote for the opponent - the incumbent has already become corrupted.

In the 2014 election, in spite of Congress having an even lower regard by the voters than the in-the-toilet rating of Obama, the electorate chose to bring back many of the incumbents to office. Apparently their feeling is that the lack of substantive progress by Congress was caused by the other guy's candidates… it was they who were the bums, not my guys/gals. This vision demonstrates how little people actually know about what their candidates are up to and what part they are responsible for in the political failures.

Holy Clinton-ism

On The Daily Show, Bill Clinton was a guest in 2008. He suggested that politicians have a really tough job, and that this is why they may be beholding to Political Action Committees (PACs). If you buy this self-serving drivel, apparently politicians have to spend most of their time flying from Washington to their home states in order to raise campaign funds, to the point of exhaustion. Well, who developed that alleged system anyway? You? Me? Hardly! It was the incumbent politicians who wanted to maintain an edge over their rivals So, that they could remain in office without having to resort to merit, even though they know that the current system is corrupt and legislatively ineffective. Should we really feel sorry for them?

If politicians wanted to correct the election process they have the power to make it happen. After all they make the laws, don't they? The reality is that reelection to office is far more important to them then is their public service. Bill's whimpering about their difficulties is nothing short of a pathetic vehicle used for creating a diversion, one which attempts to shield the politicians from their irresponsibility. My guess is that he made these statements because he did not want to be tainted by the negative truth about campaigning, or its exposure to the sleeping public.

The Election Process

Many years ago, I was asked to give a speech on any topic for a sales training course. After giving some thought to a subject matter that might not be in the mainstream, I elected to argue the merits for and against voting. It was at that point that I realized that I might not vote again. Needless to say, virtually no one in the class agreed with me on my do-not-vote side of the equation.

In spite of being repeatedly told by politicians that every vote counts, the reality is that every vote is worth (ta da) exactly one tiny vote, or virtually nothing. The pundits and politicians love to point out the one or two small town elections that were decided by a single or handful of votes as proof of their thesis.

The reason that we are constantly fed this propaganda is because it is a deliberate effort to prevent people from realizing how powerless they actually are on their couches. It does not take a mathematician to recognize that one vote out of ten million equals exactly one ten-millionth of the total number, a really miniscule fraction. When the people are told and therefore believe that they are effective in controlling the political process, then those who are actually in control can reside comfortably, unrecognized in the ether.

From another perspective, in some cases your vote may actually turn out to be worth nothing, no matter who it is cast for. It's called Super Delegate. This is where the party faithful assign themselves to a delegate status without ever being voted in by the citizens. With the Democratic Party (isn't that a misnomer), one fifth of the delegates to their recent conventions were these unelected good-ol boys and girls. They can cast their vote for any candidate that they choose, and they are responsible only to themselves. They are free to make backroom deals with whomever they choose, for their own benefit if desired.

Short of the unlikely potential of public opinion having some power over super-delegate voting, we have no controls levied upon them. Perhaps the most disturbing aspect is that when asked, these same people will defend this system in spite of its glaring injustice. This is why your one ten-millionth of the total vote may be worth zero. I assume that you appreciate standing in a long line to vote, right?

When I watch the Presidential election process (especially), there is one inescapable conclusion that comes to mind. The real power brokers must be amused at the pointless, non-issues-raising talk that constitutes the debates, speeches, and sound bites that are made by the candidates and their surrogates. Don't those who watch these charades know the difference substance and pontificating? Don't they actually know that government doesn't work, and why that is? Is there a minutia of consciousness among the voters as to who is actually running the country and what they are up to behind the scenes? The answer to all of the above questions is No!

When we don't pay attention we deserve the results that we receive. Good government is not an accident. Rather it is the result of people having knowledge and concern about its activity. The net result is that big business runs America in the background, and they do not much care who happens to get into office. They must be pleased that their control of process is seldom revealed or is obscured by those doing their bidding.

In 2008 the Democrats took control of Congress and then what? Virtually nothing changed from when the Republicans had the power. There is just more of the same old bickering to cover up the fact that all of the politicians are beholden to the same interests that throw money at both parties. And that the politicians share the same obligations to provide these businesses with their service. Could it really be any other way with our morally and ethically corrupt two-party system?

Why do you think there is so much inertia against...
* third party candidates
* government negotiated drug prices
* reasonable term limits
* a simplified tax system

Why do you think there is so much legislation that is skewed in favor of...
* investors and business - laughingly justified by the unproven trickle-down theory
* tax incentives for big oil, while they make billions of dollars in excessive profits
* loopholes for the rich that most people will never know about, much less be able to use
* subsidies that were originally designed to benefit mom and pop farms but now are mainly used to support corporate agribusiness
...and the beat goes on.

Owning Your Mistakes

There is something a little bit dysfunctional in our nature that induces us to unnecessarily cover up failures, shortcomings, and mistakes... especially for politicians. Because the press can occasionally be ruthless in its quest for sensationalism (as opposed to news) this may be an almost understandable practice. No one wants to be put in the awkward position of having to defend a reasonable past behavior by responding to the slanted interrogations of the sensation seekers. It takes valuable time and detracts from more important issues, if there were any. Even a lie will stick if it is given enough airtime. But this fact of political life does nothing to justify the wide-spread deceit and corruption that is prevalent in our elected officials.

John Kennedy took an unusual action for a politician some time ago by taking the blame for the military's Bay of Pigs fiasco in Cuba while President, even though he though it could have been attributed to a CIA intelligence failure. His mea culpa garnered him respect and contributed to a boost in his popularity. On the other hand, Richard Nixon denied his guilt in the Watergate cover-up for as long as he could and was consequently pressured into resigning in disgrace. A personality defect caused him to prefer lying to revealing his and his associates flawed and felonious judgment.

John Fitzgerald Kennedy, President: *"An error doesn't become a mistake until you refuse to correct it."*

A press-created issue a few years back involved an attack on the waterboarding of captured terrorists. In 2013 Rudi Giuliani, in a discussion regarding drone attacks, said the George Bush would not have gotten away with Obama's drone policy, as witnessed by the flack over water waterboarding. My take on this is that it only became an issue because of the administration's cover-up, not necessarily the appropriateness of the interrogation technique. Politicians don't get that lying changes everything.

In 2011 when Congresswoman Giffords was shot in Tucson, the press was quick to blame the vitriolic politicians and their own talking heads for their violence-inciting rhetoric. While I am inclined to support a degree of that logic, they went off the charts in singling out Sarah Palin (no fan of mine) for using gun-sight crosshairs on her target map of the candidates that she wanted to be defeated in the 2010 elections. Then to compound matters, her staff claimed that these icons were surveyor crosshairs. Now Sarah is a woman who lives with guns and not surveying equipment. So, rather than copping to a rather innocent use of this icon, she and her staff chose to fabricate a less than believable explanation. I guess being branded a liar by some is just part of doing business as usual.

People are generally forgiving of mistakes when the offender owns up to their gaffe and expresses contrition. When they don't, that's another matter. For politicians, the first line of defense often appears to be lying. If they had even half a brain they would know that there are no secrets for any length of time. Perhaps they rely on the public losing interest in whatever the issue was that they lied about.

While I'm referring to guns, the right wing took the position (once again) that guns don't kill people… people do. This of course flies in the face of the strong correlation between too many guns and too many shootings.

In the case of Giffords, a congressman suggested that there was no merit to limiting gun clips to ten rounds to prevent a similar carnage. He said that he would be able change to a new clip in mere seconds. This lightweight thinker conveniently ignored the fact that Gifford's shooter was tackled while trying to load another clip in his weapon.

In 2014 a similar event occurred in a public school. A hall guard tackled a shooter while he was trying to reload after shooting three students. Why can't we make the simple connection between the free flow of guns into the hands of almost anyone going hand and hand with their increasingly frequent and deadly use?

The Distraction Factor

Because Congress and the administration are all members of the same exclusive club, they will depart only So, far from being silent in order to berate a fellow colleague. Yes, they rant on over petty issues about the other party to the ears of the voters, but they do not often engage in personal or meaningful attacks against their opponents except during elections when their job survival is at stake. This restraint is a bipartisan effort at political self-preservation.

In a 2008 hearing, the head of the Justice Department was exposed for giving false testimony to a Congressional committee, which is a felony. So, did he lie? Apparently not! Did he go to jail? Not that either! Then when a same-party politician was asked to comment on the situation, instead of offering an honest opinion he responded that the person had been "inaccurate", which amounts to a lie about a lie.

Political credo: *If I don't reveal your shortcomings, you may not expose mine*.

HOW THE LAW FAILS US

The People That We Rely On For Our Protection Can Be the Biggest Offenders of It.

TABLE OF CONTENTS

Law Is For Lawyers

When there is a glitch in the legal system, lawyers are quick to defend it against all outside derision. They are known to say that the system works, in spite of occasional, glaring, abuses. It 'works', they say, because there is essentially no body with power that will correct the shortcomings So, that every user of the law gets a fair shake. It takes a major screw up for a lawyer to be censored or disbarred.

I have a number of friends who are lawyers in various categories, and some of their stories are enough to make a grown person shudder. In addition to these unfortunate tales, their attitudes towards the events do not show much empathy for those who are victimized. 'Oh well' seems to be a common theme in their thinking. Some clients will win and some clients will lose, but that does not always impact feelings and payday for the lawyers.

Let's face it. Lawyers and judges have an immense amount of power in the court room. Judges especially can make rulings that seriously affect people's lives or livelihood. While someone has to do that job, oversight on their decisions is spotty at best. Short of being overruled by a higher court on rare occasions, they get to say what goes. We have to rely on a judge's good sense and an appropriate application of the law.

From My Perspective
One of the more interesting aspects of law and justice that I have observed on the legal landscape is that the fox is in charge of the chicken coop. The preponderance of lawyers in government results in laws that suit lawyers and the judges (who are also, lawyers) who rule on laws. Curiously, while they occasionally may be involved with prosecuting conflict of interest cases, they don't seem to be aware of their own conflicted system. Or is it that they don't care to change it?

Some try to justify the preponderance of lawyers in Congress as appropriate since these are people who are making laws. Using that logic, anyone in state and city councils or on homeowner association boards should be a lawyer, because only lawyers can properly have insights and make laws. Does that half-baked train of thought have your approval? A downside to a government full of lawyers is that they come from the privileged class. And what would you think their agenda might be when it involves the wealthy vs. the poor?

Another criticism about lawyers is that they have a disincentive (conflict of interest) when it comes to settling cases in an expeditious manner. That is especially prevalent in family disputes where each side may want to punish their opponent as much as possible. Rather than forcefully suggesting mediation or binding arbitration, lawyers may be inclined to let clients unnecessarily run up their legal bills. And of course, this behavior can be manifested at the corporate level as well.

Who Is at Fault?

It is obvious that there are numerous and frequent injustices in our legal system. This is not to say that I have any special insight into the legal process that others might not have discovered. It is just that I have experienced the courts firsthand and have looked at a few of the problems that are symptomatic of a less than perfect manner in which jurisprudence is exercised in this country. What we have is a system that usually works but has glaring exceptions to the concept of justice. Well, usually doesn't get it. When power is pitted against principal, the civil rights of the weak can be subverted in favor of those who have money, status, or connections. This concept is not just a pie-in-the-sky theory, and one I will reflect on.

I recall my 20-something experience with the South Daytona Police Department. After spending time in a dance hall, my friend and I went outside to await the return of the fellow who drove us there. In spite of being both sober and quiet, a clearly red-necked cop pulled up and demanded that we get in the back of his vehicle. Vagrancy was the mumbled excuse. He then proceeded to pick up a buddy and race recklessly through the town. We ended up at the police station, which turned out to be a small, converted house with the dispatch in its kitchen. Through some miracle of chance our buddy managed to see what had happened and followed us to the station. When I saw him at the door, my release of nervous tension resulted in near hysterical laughter. To get to the punch line, we were given 24 hours to leave town.

Lawyers Required

Have you tried to secure simple regulatory advice from some city or business office clerk and been told that you needed to contact a lawyer for the answer? Organizations are So, afraid of litigation that they won't even discuss aspects of their own business without a warrant.

Or what about doctors who are prevented from revealing information about a deceased patient to the police because lawyers have made sure that they are too intimidated to act on their own? Who says that lawyers make the best judges of fair and reasonable? Even the Attorney General's office in my state will not provide any counseling beyond disclosing the wording of a particular law. So, if one wants to comprehend the implications of a law they must either be able to read gibberish to understand the statute, or (and here's the good part) hire a lawyer to do so. In my case I was attempting to determine the statute of limitation on hidden constructions defects. This is hardly a matter to require a lawyer, or so, one might imagine. Lawyers, it appears, are as interested in protecting their sources of income as they are in serving the public good.

The only relief from this unnecessary overhead can sometimes be to file an action in Small Claims court where lawyers are not required. But these matters are restricted to petty cases that are (duh) not big revenue producers for lawyers.

Our legal system's lexicon reminds me of the many years when I was a Computer Systems Analyst. Initially I was educated to use obtuse, but exact, jargon when dealing with programming. While many of the terms have become well-known today, words like megabytes, sectors, platters, software, downloading, hardwired, etc. were all alien to most folks. My dad never quite understood what it was that I did for a living.

Lawyers are also, egregious in their use of the word game. Just try to read and understand virtually any contract. Over the years I have been able to decipher much of this terminology thanks to law courses and landlord contracts, but the sheer quantity and nonsense relating to lawyer-speak is daunting. One of the excuses that you might have heard about revolves around the need for precision, but I find this to be a specious argument. My programming education (problem descriptions - facts determination - detailed instructions) requires at least as much precision in communicating an analyst's findings to a programmer, and every-day English works just fine.

Occasionally a business entity will require that their contracts be written in conversational English, but this is a rare occurrence. And without pressure from Congress (say, aren't most of them lawyers?) nothing much changes. Because there are So, few companies that require readable documents, I have to assume that their lawyers are arguing against that process. And there is no one in government who is willing to exert legalese oversight on businesses. As a landlord I come across rental documents that are designed more to obfuscate rather than inform. And these are the contracts that are being forced on lawyer-less renters.

Sir Francis Bacon: *"Information is power."*

While this quote's meaning may appear to be obvious, the full explanation is twofold...
* by know something that others do not know, you have an advantage
* obfuscate the information and you have an advantage

This gives a bit more insight into the power that information holds. Why do you think that the preponderance of our government's business is transacted unnecessarily behind closed doors, and is not often reveled to the public? Information about their activities would certainly diminish our respect for them. Say, hasn't that already happened?

White vs. Blue Collar

It's a cliché to say that white collar criminals escape their fair share of punishment. Even if they do go to jail or are convicted in civil court, their sentence is not a guarantee that justice will prevail. The original O.J. Simpson trial was a case in point. Not only did the prosecution blunder unbelievably (the [bloody, shrunken] glove did not fit So, you must acquit), but the Florida law allows retention of personal home equity making sure that Simpson paid minimal retribution for his subsequent conviction on wrongful death charges in civil court.

That state's real estate law is a liability-escape route that has been used by numerous felons because it protects their home's entire value from being confiscated by the courts. This is a classic example of how easy it is to buy law makers if you represent a major business interest. In this case, it was made possible by the Florida real estate folks as a way of generating more interest in Florida property by criminals. Much of their ill-gotten gains can be protected there by purchasing a home.

Juries are generally more sympathetic to people of higher social standing than they are to others. Blacks far outnumber the Whites in their percentage of false convictions and severe penalties. The punishment for crack cocaine, for example, is greater than for powdered cocaine only because blacks are the major users of crack.

Juries tend to vote with their genetic-emotional hearts rather than with their genetic-rational brains because they cannot easily be sympathetic to the people who have been charged with a crime or are part of another ethnic group. Emotions frequently rule the day, even though a sober, thoughtful, judgment by a jury may have been requested by the judge.

White collar crimes are viewed as being less serious then blue collar crimes which may involve violence. A person who assaults another will likely receive a harsher verdict than one who embezzles money from a company or raids a pension fund, which can cause untold anguish.

Years ago, a prominent West Coast mayor was involved in the purchase of a shipping company. Then he and his equally corrupt partners depleted the worker's pension fund before filing for bankruptcy, and they suffered no jail time for the raid. Those who were due retirement payments in their old age were the ones who suffered.

Another example of a white color crime that lacked sufficient punishment was the slick wizard of junk bonds who got five years in jail for his felonious dealings. When he was granted early released from prison, he was still a billionaire. It *pays* to have friends in high places, if you take my meaning.

The Kenneth Lay Affair

We all may know about the collapse of the Enron Corporation which was perpetrated by the actions of its executives. Because of their greed and the manufacturing of false fiscal reports, investors and employees lost some $60 billion dollars in equity when news of the corruption hit the fan.

While this may seem outrageous to most of us, it was eminently more tragic to those who saw their pensions or stock portfolios disappear in the blink of an eye. Can you imagine what it must be like to wake up one morning and learn that the income you have relied on for retirement had evaporated for good?

After too many years of litigation the Justice Department finally won their cases against Lay and his associates. Justice was served, you say. Well, not so because Lay died before the government recovered any of the restitution money. The appeals court then saw fit to vacate his conviction. The logic behind this reversal was that because of Lay's death, his estate and its lawyers would not have an opportunity to appeal the conviction since they did not have the benefit of a living defendant. Maybe you *can* take it with you.

This court's reasoning does have a semblance of logic. But in an effort to protect the rights of a perpetrator, they ignored the tragedy of victims. It's not as if...
* a jury of his peers did not convict Lay

* there had been an appeal filed for flawed court proceedings
* there were allegations of jury tampering
* there were suggestions of prosecutorial misconduct

None of the above occurred. But because of our court system, the Lay estate was permitted to retain more than $40 million in ill-gotten gains. So, his estate kept the money because they were said to be incapable of defending against the JD's conviction. Where is the logic in that? So, if you die you are not guilty, legally.

The OJ Simpson Affair

What more can be said about this despicable organism? Well, the good news is that his conviction on gun charges and kidnapping has put him behind bars for many years. What kind of sick SOB risks jail time for memorabilia? The answer is that the personal power he enjoyed for years had corrupted him ultimately.

The Scooter Libby Affair

First of all, what adult would call himself Scooter? Well, no matter. The real issue is that there had been talk in Washington and in conservative camps suggesting that he should be pardoned for his crime. And I have no doubt the high moral values of President Bush were easily subverted to find justification for that action.

Those who make an issue of their Godliness are just as likely to be offenders of it… or maybe more so

The logic against issuing a pardon to Libby went like this…
* no man is above the law
* he was convicted by a jury of his peers
* there was no injustice in his conviction
* people in power should not receive special privilege from other people in power
* we should not have a double standard for those with influence

However, these arguments apparently fell in deaf ears when it came to the ultra-conservative, right-wing elements. Integrity is not as great an issue with them when it comes to protecting a member of their peer group. While this type of behavior undoubtedly served us Well, in our long-past tribal days, it has no valid place in our current society.

This episode should send a clear message that no politician cannot be trusted to act on our behalf. So, while Bush pardoned Libby in 2007 for his crimes against the American system of justice, none of the Justice Department's evidentiary proceedings (What are the details of the crime? Why should the sentence be set aside?) were invoked prior to pardoning. It was pure politics in play.

This action will stand as testimony that Bush, like Nixon before him, was one of the most corrupt Presidents in our history. When Bush left office in 2009, his rating was in the neighborhood of 25%... an all-time low for any President. Something those in awe of him should remember.

What might learn from observing politics is that there will always be kiss-ups whose mission is to support a President's agenda and suppress evidence if asked. Like today's politics, British political history also, had its Cromwells who saw it as their duty to protect the Sovereign at any cost (but eventually it was Cromwell who took down the Crown). These protective behaviors can stem from both real and imagines threats. From another perspective, ingratiating oneself to a superior can be highly self-serving. Keeping your boss in power goes a long way toward keeping yourself in power.

Following Precedents

When it comes to judges and courts, it is the precedents that rule the day. What this means is that previous case law verdicts dictate how judges should rule or risk being overturned on appeal. Well, you may ask, how were the first cases ruled upon if there was no existing case law to refer to? The short answer is the Kings and Queens. They and their courts made the initial judgments, and because of their power their decisions could be almost as arbitrary as they saw fit. After all who was there to object… except for the church on rare occasions?

To the contrary, some of our contemporary laws have been created by judge's rulings when allowed to pass unchallenged or were upheld on appeal. Occasionally new laws are made by the appeals courts when they strike down existing law. There are also, times that laws garner new interpretations when there is a change at the bench. If a judge's legal thinking leans in a particular direction, then their judicial rulings may similarly tilt.

The law is somewhat flexible which allows judges to occasionally be attached to their own particular ideologies, just as you and I are. One positive factor that leads to judicial restraint is that the judges may find it embarrassing or their job threatened by voters if too many decisions are overturned by a higher court.

These consequences may conspire to make judges reticent to create new law even when it involves a greater justice for the complainant or defendant. Oh yes, it is the legislators who are supposed to make new law, and it is the juries who are supposed to weigh the facts. A nice theory if it completely true. But the reality is that the judges occasionally do make and reinterpret laws. At times they can even nullify a juries' decision if they find fault with it.

Winning Is Everything

Many of us may have come to the false conclusion as potential jurors that the mere fact that someone has been charged with a crime amounts to two strikes against their being innocent. Couple that attitude with a whatever-it-takes-to-win mentality of a prosecuting attorney, and you have a recipe for injustice. The case against the now-exonerated lacrosse players in North Carolina should come as a wakeup call for the judicial system (which it won't) and for the rest of us (unlikely, as well). Inertial rules.

Apparently a publicity-hungry prosecutor, who has since been disbarred, trampled on the rights of three students based solely on the dubious testimony of an alleged victim. There was no direct evidence of guilt (DNA or otherwise), and there were some strong indications that the plaintiff may have fabricated her story. Had it not been for the financial resources of the three defendants, jail time could have been assured.

In another case, Michael Morton spent 25 years being innocent behind bars because he was wrongly imprisoned for the crime of killing his wife. The government prosecutor (who has immunity from wrongdoing in office, even if it is intentional) has been accused of hiding exculpatory evidence that would have exonerated the defendant. It had finally been revealed that Michael's son told the police it was a monster who killed his mother, and it was not his father. Years down the road, a repeat offender admitted to doing the killing. Yet this was buried and not used to release the father from jail. Eventually a coalition of lawyers and ombudsmen prevailed in this case, and Morton went free.

In 2008 the late Senator Ted Stevens was convicted in a Washington D.C. federal court on charges relating to his financial disclosers. He subsequently lost his bid for reelection. Several months later the Justice Department (JD) asked the judge to vacate the conviction when it surfaced those prosecutors had withheld evidence supporting Steven's not guilty plea. A released report then said that there had been systematic concealment of exculpatory evidence that would have been corroborated his claim of innocence. This Schuelke report also, said that while inadvertent evidence-disclosure failures shouldn't occur, the JD meets its discovery obligations in nearly all cases. Well, Mr. Schuelke, nearly all doesn't really get it, does it? Perhaps his attitude would be different if he were the victim of overzealous prosecution.

The above cases and others like them raise several crucial points...
* the judicial system can be manipulated by an unscrupulous prosecutor, leaving no easy way to control that abuse
* access to money dictates how Well, or poorly one will be represented in court
* there are hundreds of people being released from prison after DNA evidence has demonstrated their innocence
* the system is far too expensive, complicated, and time consuming to be fair and balanced
* important witnesses do occasionally die before protracted trials come to a conclusion
* reasonable doubt is whatever the jurors thinks it is - or what they may be led to believe it is

In another case (James Ray/ sweat lodge deaths) the prosecution ordered the medical examiner's office <u>not</u> to testify about their finding regarding conditions at the lodge. When this was learned through discovery by the defense and the presiding judge, the trial was in jeopardy of being declared a mistrial after months of testimony. Withholding information is unconstitutional, but the prosecution wanted to win at any cost.

Winning Is Nothing

In a three-month period, I received two settlement checks from class action suits in which I was (simply by the circumstances of owning a product) part of the class. The settlements ran Well, into the multi-millions of dollars for each of the cases. My shares came to 10 and 14 *cents*.

In 2011 a major bank was confronted with a class action suit for not fully disclosing the downside of interest-only home loans to the borrowers. In the settlement, the plaintiff's lawyers were awarded $25.000.000 by a judge (being of course a lawyer) out of the $50.000.000 that was agreed to by the defendant. After this and other expenses are subtracted, the class may see only pennies here too. It's hard to be daunted at these outcomes knowing that our laws are made by and for lawyers. How bad does our legal system have to become before we insist that it be repaired?

In another nothing case, the twenty some companies who delivered their mobile home trailers to the displaced residents of Louisiana were sued because they contained dangerous amounts of formaldehyde in their products. So, a settlement was reached whereby the companies would pay fifty million dollars in fines. Why do I mention this? Because the layers take was about 50%. So, for those who have or may suffer health issues, they were paid about fifteen thousand dollars each. That's thousands vs. millions! What a grand system we have.

We all have probably noticed a number of ads on TV soliciting people to various class action causes, without disclosing as much. They say things like You may be entitled to a monetary settlement. Most recently they have begun to add a disclaimer that the speaker is a non-legal spokesperson. Why this change of dialog? Because there is nothing remotely legal about the ads in spite of featuring the names of legal firms.

So, what should we glean from these half-truths? It is apparent that the firms are doing a bit of (currently legal) ambulance chasing. That is, they are trying to gather as many victims (usually of harmful prescription drugs) as they can in order to qualify for a class action suit. When they say you might be entitled to money or some such inducement, they are merely speculating and hoping to line their own greedy pockets. By own greedy I mean that they have no serious empathy for their clients beyond the outrageous fees that they are given by the judges in this corrupt system.

Class actions suits are often nothing more than a vehicle for lawyers to get rich while the plaintiffs get pennies.

Supreme Principles

We would like to believe that the Supreme Court is composed of nine intelligent, impartial jurists who will make decisions that are equitable, reasonable and in accord with our Constitution. But if this were even half true, why would all Presidents be So, anxious to make these appointments? The answer is that members of the court come with their own political biases, and they will be selected for having attitudes that conform to the nominating President, regardless of any faithfulness to Constitutional obligations.

While it is impossible for anyone to be completely unbiased, some of us have a greater problem with this discipline than others. Judges and lawyers are typically appointed or elected for their beliefs rather than for their impartially. Presidents are known for trying to stack the court in their philosophical favor. When a like-minded candidate is installed, reinterpretation of the constitution is possible.

Fair and balanced... a fanciful flower that rarely blossoms.

An example of agenda-peddling by the Supreme Court in favor of big business came up regarding the whistleblower legislation. The court ruled 6 to 2 that a particular tattler was not entitled to recover money for his fraud exposure because he lacked "direct and independent" knowledge upon which his allegations were based. Sounds like double-talk that was designed to circumvent an important law enacted by Congress, and which serves a pressing need.

The law was passed to penalize companies involved in illegal behavior, and to encourage those who will come forward with incriminating evidence. Do we really care how they came by their information, short of breaking and entering? The method of their discovery is hardly the point. But the Court saw fit to limit the whistleblower legislation based on a business-friendly, illogical, position. Tattlers will now have less incentive to offer their service (risking termination for no profit), and the offending companies will be more immune from detection.

In another decision the Court's 5 to 4 ruling overturned a long-standing ban on companies being able to set minimum prices for the vendors of their products. This price fixing scheme had previously been legislated to be illegally anti-competitive because companies could raise the price floor for their products in concert with other suppliers. In the court's ruling, price floor setting could be either competitive (really?) or non-competitive. So, in their minds, a turn-about from the previous law was not necessarily anti-trust in nature.

Apparently the Court would have us believe that price fixing schemes can occasionally be beneficial to the consumer, but don't count on it. This decision can be seen as naked support for reduced business competition because of a counterfeit rationale. So, this Court showed how easily it ends up in the pocket of big business and antagonistic to consumers.

Curiously, there is a pricing practice that has gone unchallenged for some time in the garment industry and probably elsewhere. Not only do major suppliers to large department stores dictate the décor of the selling areas that are dedicated to their products, but they may also, tell those retailers what the selling prices will be, and how much and when the items can be marked down. Anti-trust? What else?

Recently I used the Internet in an effort to find the best price on a hepa (air purifier) filter and discovered that every seller of a particular name brand had exactly the same price... that is every seller in the US. This universal price setting is not prima-facie anti-competitive if you believe the court.

In a 2010 Court decision: Citizens United v. Federal Election Commission it struck down a provision of the McCain-Feingold election law. That law had prohibited corporations and unions from purchasing broadcast time for election matter that named a candidate within 30 days of a primary and 60 days of a general election. This decision freed up corporations and unions to spend unlimited amounts on electioneering communications. In addition, the donors were not required to be identified. The rationale behind this change was that most of this type of political spending occurs outside of contributions to a candidate's campaign, and as such the campaigns were not accountable for the veracity or lack of such with the communications. Really? What it did require is that there must be a wall between these Super PACs and the campaigns they favor. This is, of course, a flight of fantasy since that activity cannot easily be controlled when it is done surreptitiously.

And there is no firewall in place which would prevent communications with candidates by Super PACs. In 2012 John McCain said: "I predict to you that there will be scandals associated with this huge flood of money". The justification by the Court was that their decision was based on freedom of speech principles. Did they ever think about balancing probable corruption against the interests of the people?

The classic analogy in opposition to this ruling is the prohibition against yelling fire in a theatre. And then there is the undeniable consideration that this money will be flowing from the super-rich in concert with *their* interests, which are unlikely to be those of the rest of us. Could the court be any more wrong-headed?

In 2006 the Court ruled that is was not illegal for telecommunications companies to cooperate with National Security Agency's warrant less eavesdropping on internal telephone conversations and email. Some 30 suites had been filed since that information became public. To its discredit, the Court upheld the previous decision in 2012.

To its credit, the Court did rebuke the Bush administration for years of stonewalling on acknowledging global warming. The EPA had presented the Court with a list of irrelevant (to the point of being ludicrous) reasons why they declined to take action on automobile and truck emissions. One of the more specious arguments was that auto pollution is not deemed to be poisonous. That's news to me. How about you?

Maybe these deep thinkers were standing behind someone's tailpipe for too long. More likely it is that the bureaucrats owed their allegiance to the administration instead of to the public.

Then in its wisdom the EPA suggested that this matter should be resolved by a voluntary approach (haven't we heard that nonsense before), rather than by regulation. I believe we know how proactive and inclined toward making changes for the better the auto industry has been throughout the years. Not!

The ruling was 5 to 4 in favor of a critical environmental issue… one that should have been a 9-zip slam-dunk. This split should make us wonder what the agenda of the opposition judges was. Perhaps the Court's philosophy is all about not restraining big businesses on whatever they deem to be in its interest, as opposed to what is in the best interest of consumers.

Gettysburg Redress

In 2012 the Court affirmed the law that allows corporations to give unlimited contributions to political parties. While the decision was not unanimous, it was unfortunate. In upholding an oblique reference to the Constitution regarding free speech, the Court ignored the damage to free politics. Their ruling was like giving all of the hotels to one of the players in Monopoly and then expecting a fair game. What it did do is give those contributors with big bucks at their disposal another avenue to corrupt the already corrupted Congresspersons.

What we end up with this decision is an inclination to paraphrase Lincoln with: Government of the corporations, by the corporations, and for the corporations. I suppose that this is not all that bad for many Republicans.

End of Book

HOW THE PRESS FAILS US
What They Do & How They
Contribute To Bad Government

Table of Contents

Pride and Prejudice

I'm going to lump the press into the same category as big business because they walk the walk and talk the talk. Ergo they are indeed big business. In stark contrast to my personal opinion, reporters might imagine themselves as being…

* independent members of the fourth estate (a coined phrase by Edmund Burke during a parliamentary debate in 1792 on the opening up of press reporting in the House of Commons in England)
* guardians against government evils
* purveyors of the truth

In addition we have reporters and commentators coddled to the point where their egos bloom, and they feel that they can determine what the rules of proper reporting should be. As an example of egos out of control, one news program claims to broadcast from the situation room. Really? Isn't this so-called room where the President and his advisors make global decisions?

In reality their reporting more often finds them in the categories of both government collaborators and show business outlets. By this I mean that their performance is often directed at facilitating political deceit and pandering to sensationalism, as much as it is toward probing for and providing pertinent news.

I mention the delinquency of the press many times, and with good justification. They may fancy themselves as watchdogs, but it is not difficult to tell that the reality and cultivated images are far different.

During elections, voters are seldom given the kind of information that could help them make informed decisions. Instead of this they are bombarded with air time from and about candidates that spin the truth, rather then enlighten us.

And the press is just as adept at spin as are the politicians. Their op-eds are filled with opinions, attitudes, and disparagements that show little regard for facts. Even having their errors and false insinuations brought to light does not stop the prevarication if commentators think they can gain an additional mile out of a false statement.

Adding insult to injury, broadcasts are filled with commercials and teasers (you know… the stay tuned for whatever) to the point of distraction. We are routinely bombarded with these coming attractions that are injected at the end of a news segment to peak our interest and keep us from changing stations. If we want the details about an issue that was mentioned, we must endure the commercial delay, then wait for the second or third segment down the road before the promised information is presented. Occasionally the teaser occupies more time then does that actual information.

During the 2008 Presidential campaign, one of the talking heads at a round table discussion conceded that he and his fellow reporters were responsible for creating a candidates momentum or loss of the same. This was acknowledged while displaying a look of pride. Interestingly there was no objection from the other journalists at this affair. So, it is clear that they know the truth about their manipulation of the public, and they may not much care to correct it.

It is reasonable to assume that one of the presses primary roles should be to ask probing questions to reveal the truth, and expose dishonesty. Personal biases ought to be left at home and not be incorporated into the shading of their reporting. Far too often this is wishful thinking.

Let me demonstrate common press biases by first analyzing the appropriate technique for interrogating a witness in our courts…
* unless the judge permits a lawyer to treat a defendant as hostile, questions that are accusatory may not be allowed

* questions may not begin with leading or assumption-directed phrases like Isn't it true that -or- Didn't you…
* rather, the phrasing must be Is it true that -or- Did you…

These rules of conduct should similarly be used by members of the press as a proper method for keeping their agendas out of the questioning. However it is not the least bit unusual to have reporters express their personal beliefs couched in their queries because there is no one to stop them… certainly not their bosses who must surely encourage the behavior.

Attitude peddling puts the press in the position of making or tainting the news, rather than just reporting on it. One motivation behind the presses methods of questioning can be explained as a tawdry effort to interject sensationalism into the reporting process because this is what viewers/readers want. As a result, we get what we ask for.

An unbiased press is a nice theory, but it is not the norm. To demonstrate this absence of straight forward reporting we might ask ourselves….
* Do the media outlets have an obvious preponderance of liberal or conservative columnists on their staffs?

* Are their news stories slanted in a particular direction without an accurate representation of both sides on each issue?
* Do they voice expressed or implied support for one candidate or issue over another?
* Do the reporters ask leading, rather than probing questions?
* Are they inclined to be neutral?

Presses Inclinations

One of the proclivities of the press is to report on an event or topic using the term reportedly in order to attach a hint of veracity to a news story. What exactly does reportedly mean? It may mean that someone wishes to remain anonymous, and still be able to pass along confidential information to a reporter. However this in no way implies that the disclosed facts have veracity.

Or it may be the quoted person's method of poisoning the waters of an opponent. Additionally it may be used to deflect attention from an issue. Far too often reporters uses this ruse to get newsprint or air time. In point of fact, the press is less exacting with the truth than are most of us. After all they are paid by the word and not necessarily by a thought's merits or its authenticity. Why do you think the press drones on endlessly over stories that deserve less than a passing glance?

Did we really need…
* six days of news about President Ford's funeral
* the months of bylines regarding a college sex scandal
* the endless rant about the death of a wife by her playboy husband
* an obsession with the Congressperson who groped his staff members
* focusing on Congresspersons who cheat on their mates (which is immoral) rather than their voting records (which can also, be immoral).

And don't think that the anniversary of each traumatic event from recent history will escape there attention either. Nothing much has changed with Charles Manson in a quarter of a century, but he still hits the news on an annual basis. Where would the press be without a tickler file?

The press can be So, preoccupied with the specter of tasteless sensationalism because there is a ready audience for this kind of foolishness… called yellow journalism. No horrific story is allowed to go under reported. One of the channels in my area goes So, far as to dedicate most of their evening news budget to as many police blotter stories (murder, rape, pedophiles, hit and run) as they can locate.

Do we really learn anything valuable from this type of reporting? It certainly does not uncover what our politicians have failed to accomplish while they are in office due to their conflicted, money raising, activities. But those disclosures would require real reporting, which is not in most reporters' playbooks.

Mark Twain, author: "If you don't read the newspaper you are uninformed, if you do read the newspaper you are misinformed."

News By Assassination

Now that cable television has become a major medium for the dissemination of news, we are inundated with the talking heads who both create and exploit controversy. They may express personal and occasionally vitriolic opinions, perhaps more than they present news. They drone on endlessly with tawdry attitudes that fill the airwaves and use tortured logic in an effort to make political hay for their favored issue, party or candidate.

Because of this failure to be impartial, we should ask...
* How dare reporters and networks align themselves into liberal and conservative camps anyway?
* Is that the best way to present the news and inform the public?

* Can't we find people with a balanced point of view and no political ax to grind?
* Shouldn't we insist on honesty and integrity from the news media?

On both the ultra-conservative and ultra-liberal sides of the spectrum we have a string of commentators (notice that I did not say reporters) who seem to relish the limelight that they have created for themselves. Why else would they be invited to visit the late night variety shows if they weren't in show business? And this celebrity is accomplished at the expense of unbiased reporting.

While a few may make an effort to present the news in a relatively impartial fashion, the majority are preoccupied with casting aspersions on their targets as often as they can manage without being too redundant. This contrived melodrama takes the format of...
* innuendo
* exaggeration
* distortion
* out of context quotes (especially)
* deliberate misinterpretation
* outright lies

I guess the current king of deliberate misrepresentation is Sean Hannity on the Fox channel, perhaps only because I do not listen to the radio talk shows. His biases can be So, blatant and irrational that they have become annoying to listen to, which is a long way from being informative. Essentially he has cast himself as a rabble rouser with only a passing concern for the truth. Often that infrequent truth is couched among half-truths and what must surely be intentional lies.

Corporations that employ these personalities do so, not for the straightforward presentation of news and the accuracy of their statements, but for the ratings that they seek to achieve. Audiences will believe almost anything if it is presented with enough conviction, emotion, authority, and repetition. And these news stories may continue to surface until Well, after the incidence has been debunked by legitimate authority.

So, how does just flirting with the truth succeed in this country? The answer may be lumped under the heading Validation Journalism. What that means is that people tend to listen to those programs and politicians that conform to their way of thinking. What this also, means is that they may not be very interested in examining competing points of view. If they were So, inclined, the flood of predominately, single-minded liberal and conservative programs would have less chance of occupying the air-waves.

In years gone by the three major network anchors appeared to disseminate a relatively dispassionate view of the daily news. In fact as a child I had wished for those programs were more revealing or controversial, especially when it came to news about the politicians. But in a classic case of be careful what you wish for, that tide has turned. Much of the prrogramming that passes for news has an entertainment quality, and an occasionally nasty quotient to it.

In 2013 Obama gave his State of the Union address. This was followed by the Republican reply, as has become the tradition. Marko Rubio was tapped as the up-and-comer in the ranks to deliver the opposition's message. During his speech he leaned awkwardly to retrieve a bottle of water and take a sip. No big deal, right? Wrong. The in-Obama's-pocket media turned the uncomfortable movement into a mini-indictment of Marko. So, when the press wants to degrade someone, they will not hesitate to pick on anything that they can get away with.

The social reporting on celebrities is even worst. Do we really need to care about the out-of-control lives of these pampered, self-centered, brats? A case in point about slanted coverage would be the initial fifteen minute apology of Tiger Woods regarding his extra-marital affairs.

While my wife and I thought that his contrition was reasonably on point, members of the blather media generally gave him poor marks for reading a prepared speech and for not taking any question.

Like little children who wanted to play with someone else's toy, the press felt that Tiger selfishly took control of the event. It did not matter that he responded to the questions on the minds of most people. He was berated by the media types for not giving them their fair share of time. Could that criticism be any more revealing of how they see themselves as being entitled? Talk about arrogance.

In the ninety days prior Tiger's TV appearance, the celebrity press was involved in hundreds, perhaps thousands of hours devoted to dissecting his personality, personal life, and illicit behavior. Their opinions were not labeled as such, but they were presented as valid insights by those in the know. The truth is that these commentators demonstrated virtually nothing beyond wild guesses, assumptions, and fabrications.

In an interesting addendum to the above, the press saw fit to interview at least one of the women who were involved in affairs with Tiger. The person that I saw being given her fifteen minutes of shame lamented the fact that Tiger did not apologize to her since he had said that he loved her. Could this person possibly be even more self-absorbed than Tiger? He was married, you know. How does she figure that her rights were abridged? Did she ever think about the rights of Tiger's wife? Sounds like a sleazy bar-broad to me.

Creating the Issues

Rarely does the national TV press ignore an opportunity to criticize a candidate for changing their mind on a major issue... flip-flopping as they are inclined to call it. We should all appreciate that life and circumstances are constantly in a state of flux, and that only the most stubborn person would not be willing to learn a new lesson when the opportunity comes along. Yet the incident-creation types that wield the airwaves would have us believe that taking a new stance more often than once in a blue moon indicates a fatal lack of integrity.

According to the press, if we cannot believe what is said on some date forever, than how could we ever believe any other things that the candidate has said? This is either...
* a fool's logic
* a shallow effort to impugn someone's veracity without any real justification
* a shameless attitude that makes for good press

At a political rally in 2007 John McCain made a modest joke by paraphrasing the Beach Boys' song "Barbara Ann". He devilishly changed a refrain to: Bomb Iran. It was more interesting than funny, but the press invented a seamy side to the lyrics and tried to make an issue of it. McCain's appropriate and quick response was that they "Lighten up and get a life". It was nice to see someone refuse to back down to the sensation seekers that have found a home in the press corps. That demonstrated how desperate some reporters are to get their fifteen seconds of air time to protect their job security.

I can imagine that the newspaper's daily editor/reporter meetings are not only filled with quasi-intellectual talk about which of the stories are more important than others, or which deserve the front page of the paper, or first position on the TV news broadcast. They must also, discuss how to sensationalize them for the public appetite because that is what people want. If this were not true, there would not be dozens of pages and hours of television devoted to the latest campus shooting or missing child. How does a campus shooting differ from the hundreds of other shootings that may occur daily? The answer may be: wealthy, white-collar offspring.

When we want legitimate sensationalism, the press is mostly mute. We know little of what is happening in Iraq and Afghanistan, which are government controlled news venues. There is seldom a mention of how much those countries people may be suffering or (especially) why they blame Americans for much of that sorrow. After all, we need to be viewed by ourselves as the good guys. And the press corps has no incentive to upset that particular applecart because they feed off it.

To get into the reasons why Arabs may blame us for their difficulties, we have to try to understand their mindset. They…
* are religious in the extreme
* do not co-exist Well, with other religions
* can label non-Arabs as infidels
* believe that their homeland is only their land
* will not tolerate invaders (which can be everyone else)
* would rather live under religious tyranny than under democratic oppression because this is their culture
* dismiss freedom as a political con that is played on the Europeans and Americans
* might rather be blown up than submit to Western ideas
* believe that an honorable death is to be revered and not feared

* think we are too stupid to go home (ok, on this last point they have my full agreement)

Does any of the above make sense to you? These arguments against staying the Middle East do not seem to sway more than a handful of our politicians.

Press Promotions

The press is not with out guilt in manufacturing those false heroes which we may have come to admire. For example, when a President dies, the only people who are asked to bear witness about his presidency and persona to the media are the deceased's friends and well-wishers. Had I not been aware of Presidential behaviors that frequently have been dishonorable, I might be moved by this contrived adulation.

It is not my intention to personally denigrate Gerald Ford and George Bush… just to note that they were under-qualified office holders. Likable or not, the job of being President was substantially over their heads, as Gerry once conceded. And Ford performed a disservice to the country when he preemptively pardoned Richard I am not a crook Nixon, the de facto leader of the Watergate felons.

Lately the wags are giving Ford high marks for this intervention in that justice process as being responsible for putting an unfortunate event behind us. So, with this logic, should we let all felons out of prison because it degrades our image? Even today President Nixon, the preeminent poster boy for: corrupt government starts at the top is being forgiven by the press for his…

* enemies list
* paranoia
* shady dealings
* direct association with felons
* being an un-indicted conspirator

Press Passivity

We apparently have short memories when it comes to recalling the negative aspects in our political history as they relate to our Presidents. Or perhaps we just can't stand to think of them as the felons that they occasionally are. Do you remember when President Johnson had a juicy broadcast license for an Austin radio station delivered to his wife Lady Bird in spite of the intense competition for that plum? Did the press have more than a passing reference or two to this event?

Prior to Nixon's journey into infamy, his aids were putting out feelers about having him nominated for a Nobel Peace Prize. This was ostensibly justified by his ending the Viet Nam war and ordering our troops home. So, the mere act of stopping an illegitimate policy of President Johnson was purported to make a world hero out of him.

Does anyone wonder just how Nixon's aids thought that they might be successful with their Peace Prize promotion? And aren't you just a little bit curious about what putting out feelers implies? Perhaps it means that they thought the Nobel committee could be manipulated in some way. Another explanation might be that the mere mention of Nixon and Nobel in the same breath would enhance his image for the next election.

Does all of this slight of hand mean that we have not had a number of respect-worthy Presidents? No. But perhaps there were more in our early history rather than these later years.

It does not necessarily follow that our most-revered Presidents had carried out their duties all that Well, in spite of positive press reporting. Americans just like to have our heroes regardless of whether or not it makes sense or is accurate. It is all part of the Indian and chief genetics that sanctions our respect for leaders even though it is out sync with their abilities or integrity.

Because of our gullibility, government officials can and do lie to us with impunity, and suffer few consequences from the charade.

Who Is In Charge?

Subsequent to the lawsuit that was filed by Dan Rather against CBS in 2007 it became evident that the press's practice of improper reporting goes Well, beyond its reporters. If one can put their faith in Dan's contention about CBS management, the executives that own the news outlets are also, responsible for misshaping the news. Their pressure to suppress or slant stories amounts to censorship, just as much as leaving out pertinent details or ignoring obvious conclusions would.

Dan related to an inquiry that the documents which would have condemned Bush's unmilitary-like military record, and the opportune loss of same, had not been conclusively demonstrated to be either accurate or inaccurate. They were just conveniently missing. Yet CBS was alleged to have forced Dan into an on-air apology in order to maintain good relations with the White House. So, one has to ask, do we really want news outlets cultivating cozy relations with the same government entities that they are supposed to be reporting on? Do we want the chickens hanging out in the foxes den and doing their bidding?

The Presses Role

The epidemic-level of political malfeasance that is part and parcel of public office is made possible thanks to (ta da) the average folks who want to believe the best about their elected officials, and who seldom question what mischief that they may be up to. This applies equally to the press because they can occasionally be up to no good as well. For example, the reporters are less than critical of the...

* political press handouts which may be accepted as gospel
* politician's statements that are generally taken at face value
* evasive answers that are allowed to go unchallenged
* luxurious, taxpayer-paid, press-tag-along trips with Presidents that go lightly reported
* shameful debates that go on in Congress

Another aspect of the under-reported behavior that occurs while in office is the sense of entitlement that is demonstrated by elected officials. Take Obama for example. Those who are fortunate enough to travel with the President on mind-numbingly-expensive jaunts around the globe are seldom critical of the cost, even though they should be fully aware of it. The perk is just too good to pass up in spite of the manipulative effect it has on reporters.

Another White House directed exploitation of the press is the elite reporters who are being invited to party at cozy press events with the same officials they may be assigned to report on. And of course they want to be invited back for the next up-close-and-personal gala by limiting their aggressive reporting. This is not exactly the arm's length arrangement that the forth estate should establish for themselves.

The difference between reporters and automobile salespeople is that we all know that the later are deceitful.

Yes, the press does provide a few stories that may expose some of the questionable behaviors of politicians, but this is usually done without crossing the line of press etiquette. When these disclosures do occur, reporters may be exposing just the tip of the iceberg with their limited follow-up. Or they may be mostly picking on those whose behaviors are over the top. If the press corps were only marginally aggressive in their reporting they could fill the news with political activity for which you and I might go to jail.

In 2009 New Jersey sting operation, the feds netted dozens of high ranking officials, including some Mayors, who were indicted for corruption. Yet until the feds revealed these arrests, the dealings of this band of alleged felons were virtually unknown to the public. If you can have this many persons involved in an active conspiracy to subvert government it should not have come as a complete surprise. After all how did the feds conclude that something was wrong if there was no smoke around this fire? So, where was the press when the conspiracy was going down?

Another of the press's gifts that are bestowed on politicians is the allowing a lack of attribution by the government's rules-makers about their pronouncements and dictates. There is hardly a day that goes by without a press story assigning credit to some nameless, faceless, element, such as...
* the Pentagon said this
* the VA refused to do that
* the State Department did this
* the Justice Department decided not to pursue...

Well, who exactly are there anonymous people any way? I am fairly sure that the government buildings do not make our public policy. Because we rarely learn the names of those who are responsible for our government's actions, decision making is conveniently protected by this veil of secrecy. Others in a position to know the inside story may have their own jobs to protect. Consequently they may be disinclined to risk any retribution with an ill-advised revelation. The result of this secrecy is that bureaucrats are relatively free to set policies and practices that may be in conflict with the public good.

Do you remember when the press dutifully reported those trumped-up stories about the remains of Iraqi chemical factories being discovered in dilapidated tractor trailers for example? Right! Our countries chemical factories occupy hundreds of acres, but those clever, sandal-footed, Iraqis were So, sophisticated that they could produce nerve gases in dirty, non-air-conditioned truck trailers in the middle of the desert.

Then there was VP Cheney's subsequent role in the manufactured WMD stories which his office blamed on other agencies for an information failure. Had the press corps and Congress been more diligent (say at the sixth grade level) we wouldn't be killing Americans in a country that wants no part of us and has So, little regard for their own lives.

Our militaristic attitude may have been somewhat encouraged by the memberships of Bush, Cheney, Rice, and Rhumsfeld in The Project for the New American Century, a non-profit, educational organization dedicated to a few fundamental propositions. Among their platforms are the beliefs that…

* American leadership is good for both America and for the world
* such leadership requires military strength, diplomatic energy, and commitment to moral principle
* we should rally support for a vigorous and principled policy of American international involvement

Now that the truth about the war had somewhat come to light, is it any wonder why Cheney chose not to test the political waters, much less run for President? Oh yes, and what became of the exposé of his previous company, Halliburton, and the allegations about their misappropriation of hundreds of billions of dollars from the war's reconstruction effort. And why were fees still being paid to them to help restore Iraq when that story was exposed? Where was the press follow-up on this alleged theft of taxpayer money?

When there is no press accountability of officials, there is corruption.

Press and Context

What may arguably be the worst case of the press's penchant for ruthlessly taking people's words and intent out of context is the controversy that erupted in 2008 regarding Reverend Wright and Barak Obama. Because

Wright had expressed his frustration with the establishment in highly excessive terms, he was derided by the press in a most uncharitable manner. There is little doubt this came about only because Barak was a parishioner in the Reverend's church, and would not have received any attention otherwise.

While I do not understand Wright's rant about the government creating aids to control blacks and other odd statements, I judged his "God damn America" refrain to mean God damn the government for not making America color blind. You may not like the words he chose, but it would be hard to argue with the intent behind them, if I got it right.

Wright's later speech before the NAACP, however, could not have been more inspiring. Perhaps it was the speech of the decade regarding race relations, and one that will surely be ignored for years. His argument was that Blacks being different is not the same thing as Blacks being deficient, referring to the way in which African Americans are sometimes cast because of their local speech patterns. He went on to say that we are all different in a variety of ways and no one should be labeled as inferior because of that. I would challenge anyone to read his speech and come away without having that understanding reinforced.

But the ever vigilant press jumped at the opportunity to repeatedly broadcast a few maliciously chosen, out of context phrases with which to condemn him. They apparently could not resist their prime directive which is to indulge in trivialization and sensationalism whenever possible.

Wright's examples of discrimination against Blacks was to repeat two Well, known Presidential quotes in his poorly attempted accents of Kennedy and Johnson. He went on to point out that they had not been demeaned for communicating in their regional tongues. But when Blacks converse in their dialect they are put down as inferior.

So, how did the press present this to the public? Almost unbelievably they extracted the two phrases in such a way as to portray Wright as mocking Kennedy and Johnson, which by anyone's reading was not his intention. Then armed with their own distorted reporting, they went on to disparage Wright as a vindictive person and someone who may have been out to damage Obama. Talk about creating news from nonsense.

I have no evidence to show that the press was attempting to do Obama a favor by allowing him to further distance himself from Wright, but they certainly maligned Wright for some reason. Maybe it was just another case of creating fodder for the sensationalism-hungry public.

American Monarchy

While presidential excesses are by no means limited to Obama, he has set a new benchmark for over the top travel spending. It is not just foreign royalties that fly with a fleet of luxurious jets to far off destinations for a few hours rather than using the phone to conduct their business. Are you aware that his frequent travels include...
* a second jumbo jet for the press (So, that they keep their mouth's under control?) and other VIPs?
* several planes for the President's many vehicles and staffers
* airplanes to bring in gasoline tanker trucks for the President's planes to guarantee that the fuel is not tampered with
* contingents of anti-terrorist military located along motorcade routes
* copious supplies - ranging from lighting, to red carpets, and speaker stands, which are just the tip of equipment-iceberg
* Michelle Obama taking her hairdresser (can she no longer comb her own hair?), along with a large contingent of superfluous staffers, aboard Air Force One trips, with nary a peep from the press

* vacation trips to Hawaii that have been reported to cost taxpayers about $1.5 million per week
* a trip was made to Africa in order to underscore the President's commitment to malaria containment (I guess the phones were down that day)
* in the first weeks of the nuclear problem in Japan, Obama played golf and took his family on a trip to Brazil. Does that remind anyone of the Bush's lack of proper reaction to Katrina?

In the election year of 2012 Obama used the travel resources of the White House to make various trips to swing states at the taxpayer's expense. The House Speaker, Boehner, criticized these trips as merely political, which if true they must, by federal law, be paid for by Obama's election campaign. One of the trips was said to be nothing more than a fake fight with Congress regarding federally funded student loan rates.

The President has the resources of regular press events at which he could easily voice his concerns, either directly or through the White House press office. So, we end up paying millions of dollars for his lavish trips which are purely political in nature, and then the President lies (implicitly and explicitly) about their need for the public benefit… obviously without remorse over their costs. The entitled persons can never spend too much to become embarrassed, apparently.

All of the above reminds me of the television program American Greed where the felons show no concern for the people that they fleece.

Knowledge Suppression

Information that the public should become aware of is occasionally suppressed by the news media, politicians, corporations, and government agencies because it is in their interest to do so. This distortion occurs because…
* the news media is beholding to the politicians and agencies who feed them propaganda
* government agencies are obligated to politicians who fund their money-wasting bureaucracies
* politicians are indebted to the large corporations who pull the strings with their campaign financing (bribes)
* large corporations are obliged to… Well, to no one actually because they are truly the owners of government

The free press is not really So, free, is it.

These circumstances add up to the incestuous relationships that conspire to suppress meaningful information from being disclosed to the public and from beneficial laws from being passed. Perhaps the most infamous of these naked suppressions took place a few years back when Ralph Nader was making a run for President. The press would only give disparaging lip service to his candidacy, and then just as often it would misrepresent his views. The press encouraged us to believe that a vote for Ralph was a wasted vote, and that it was tantamount to a vote for the Republicans because most of Nader's supporters would have been inclined to vote Democratic.

The information controllers went So, far as to prevent Nader from joining the Presidential debates in the 2000 election. Third party candidates were deemed to be detrimental to democracy, and they were viewed as being a liability to a stable two-party system. Third party candidates may indeed be injurious to our political system because they foster the presentation of new ideas, and they may not permit politicians hide behind their Coke vs. Pepsi subterfuge.

Not too surprisingly the debates referred to above were run by officials from the Republican and Democratic national committees, not by the organization that stood in as their stalking horse, the Daughters of the American Revolution (DAR). That group was used to put an independent face on what was a patently bipartisan conspiracy. Shame on the DAR for getting its fifteen minutes of shame by being manipulated this manner!

When Ralph Nader arrived at one of these debates with a valid ticket for a seat in the audience, the thought-police refused him entry into the auditorium, and threatened him with arrest if he insisted on taking a seat. His picture, and those of the others who were cast as enemies of the convention, had been placed in the so-called Book Of Faces.

The politicians and the interests that were behind this restriction of free assembly could not risk any breach in the wall of secrecy which prevents disclosure of who is truly running this country. Interfering with the tightly controlled, two-party system might uncover that fact to the masses, they correctly reasoned. This control of process is only marginally less obnoxious than that which occurs in the banana republics that we have criticized for such activity.

Getting back to Nader, the Democrats to this day claim that his running for the Presidency in 2000 caused Al Gore to lose the election to George Bush, and they are still pissed at him. While I obviously am not a fan of GWB, I am less disposed to the arguments against Nader. It is disappointing that So, few people had a clue as to his justifications for running. His platform was designed to put up an offence against the pervasive influence that big business has on our legislators due to legalized bribery.

While that message does not seem difficult to grasp, it did none the less fail to capture much of an audience. If the Democrats could not distinguish themselves enough to overcome the less than one percent of the vote that was received by this third party, then perhaps they deserved to lose.

We should know by now that no matter whom the candidates may be, are our choices are always between twiddle dee dee and twiddle dee dum. Voting for candidates merely validates those who choose to corrupt them, this country, and deceive the voters.

One of the arguments that is perpetually put forward against voting for a third-party candidate is that it represents a lost vote because that party has no chance of winning. Well, what about the contention that that a useless vote sends an important message of discontent. And who says a third party cannot move up in stature?

Hasn't the formation of the TEA party managed to influence some Republican candidates? Currently our populous is not disenchanted enough with the current state of politics to take the third-party step. This is no doubt because we have been indoctrinated since birth into believing that the current system works. Could we be more wrong? Wasn't the 2011 budget fiasco a wake-up call, even for those asleep on their couches?